The Divine Trilogy Of Sarah Bernhardt

The Beginning,
The Middle,
And The End
Of A Theatrical Legend

Three Plays by
Robert W. Cabell

WP
Warrington Press
Renton Washington and Brooklyn New York

THE DIVINE TRILOGY OF SARAH BERNHARDT

As Produced in reparatory at:

The Trilogy Theater
341 West 44thStreet
New York, NY 10036
In 2001

No part of these scripts may be used or reproduced by any means, graphic, electronic, or mechanical: including photocopying, recording, taping, or by any information storage retrieval system, without the written permission of the publisher, except in the case of brief quotations embodied in critical articles and reviews.

Warrington Publications may be purchased through booksellers or by going to www.WarringtonPress.com.

Copyright 2013. All rights reserved.

ISBN: 978-0-9889698-6-5 (hardcover)
ISBN: 978-0-9889698-5-8 (paperback)

Printed in the United States of America.

DEDICATED TO

Pi Douglas and Peter McLean who make up my own divine trilogy of friends and collaborators.

THE DIVINE RISING STAR

PART I OF THE DIVINE TRILOGY OF SARAH BERNHARDT

THE LIFE AND TIMES OF SARAH BERNHARDT

A Play Robert W. Cabell

Directed by Pi Douglas

A One Woman Show
as Performed by Darlene Troiano

THE DIVINE RISING STAR

Produced in reparatory at:

The Trilogy Theater
341 West 44thStreet
New York, NY 10036
In 2001

No part of this script may be used or reproduced by any means, graphic, electronic, or mechanical: including photocopying, recording, taping, or by any information storage retrieval system, without the written permission of the publisher, except in the case of brief quotations embodied in critical articles and reviews.

THE DIVINE RISING STAR

is dedicated to

my niece, Kelsey, who wants and has
all the talent she needs to be Divine,
and
to my other divine nieces,
Krysten, Caitlyn, and Kelli.

CHARACTER

SARAH BERNHARDT: The mother of Sarah Bernhardt, her aunt, and two sisters were all known for their great beauty and were celebrated courtesans of Paris. Sarah herself was considered thin and plain, but with an exceptionally rich and melodious speaking voice. Her reddish-blonde hair was thick, frizzy, and unruly, her arms overly long, her bust too small, and her nose too big. Yet when she walked onstage in the character of one of her fallen women, she imbued herself with a radiance and internal war of emotions that transformed her into the pinnacle of style and sensuality. She was the first woman to successfully portray the male role of Hamlet, and the only actress to receive rave reviews for both the roles of Hamlet and Ophelia.

Bernhardt embraced a personal life that was equally daring and dramatic. She slept in a coffin, traveled with a menagerie of wild and exotic animals, including panthers, rhinos and pythons, was the first woman to ride in a hot air balloon, hunted bears and crocodiles, and had a love of all things strange and macabre. Her onstage love scenes were equally matched by her torrid affairs, well into her 70's. Most of her leading men were her lovers, and her closest personal friend was a notorious lesbian. That combined with her sold out, salacious performances, made her the most famous woman in the world for over half a century.

Sarah was anti-drugs, anti-smoking, and vehemently against the death penalty in an era when civilization accepted all of those. Her circle of intimate friends included the greatest writers of her time, like Oscar Wilde, Alexander Dumas, Victor Hugo, Mark Twain, and royalty such as, Edward the Prince of Wales and his wife Princess Alexandra. The Czar of Russia knelt to her, a Belgium prince fathered her only child, and the Grand Duke of Austria vacated his castle for her use. President Teddy Roosevelt was a devoted fan, as well as some of the greatest intellectuals of her time such as, Edison, Tesla, and Freud.

At fifty she was convincingly portraying nineteen year old virgins, and her romantic scenes were both the rage and scandal of the civilized world. Dying on stage slowly, tortuously, languidly, and tragically, was her greatest specialty.

Those who came after her desperately tried to mimic her poses and gestures which were organic to her unique talents. Those who mimicked her were judged as overly dramatic or cliché. No audience that saw Bernhardt "die," escaped the onslaught of the deep and overwhelming emotions she conveyed.

SETTING

The set has three basic areas. Down stage left is a gilded French vanity with a gold framed mirror on the vanity which is scattered with bottles and boxes and jewelry, with a silver brush and comb set.

Stage left of the vanity is an exotic looking full length carved tri-folding mirror. It has inset panels of fur, and shells inset in various patterns around the recessed mirrors.

On the upstage right side of the vanity (no more than two or three steps away), is an elegant and lavishly dressing screen decorated with Sarah's theatrical posters designed by Muca with some of her greatest roles. Draped over the edges of the dressing screen are a Kimono, a hooded floor-length velvet cape, and various, shawls, scarves and gloves. Hooked on top to the far stage right side of the screen are two or three hats of various sizes. Directly in front of the dressing screen to one side is a large brass umbrella stand. Inside are parasols, a sword and scabbard, and an African death stick from New Orleans,(a tall wooden staff with a carved human skull on top.)

Upstage center is a divan, or fainting couch draped in red brocade. Various sizes of pots and vases full of flowers are on either side of the divan both on the floor and on top of stacks of books and baskets. Two mismatched elegant side tables with picture frames, and crystal decanters frame the divan. On a silver tray is a crystal goblet, that Sarah will fill and drink from the decanters throughout the show. This is an essential element for the actress to keep her voice in shape and should be worked into the staging of the show.

The wall has gilded framed theatrical posters and paintings of Sarah, and collections of masks and artifacts from many different countries and cultures. In front of the Divan is a battered wooden traveling chest, with a leopard skin fur shawl draped to one side. The other side has a large brass hand fan with peacock feathers. Throughout the show Sarah will, take things from the trunk, sit or even stand up on it.

Far down stage right is an open space that is framed in front by a half circle of brass antique foot lights. Far upstage and directly behind this open area is a white scrim, framed across the top and draped to the floor on either side by classic style dark red velvet drapes. It gives the effect of a small proscenium arch and when Sarah recreates most of her famous monologues they will begin or end in this space. The white scrim area is used for projections of clouds during the hot air balloon monologues and projections of the images of war.

COSTUMES

Sarah wears a long simple full length sleeveless white sheath. During the show she will accessories it with various shawls, scarves, capes, hats, gloves, Parasol, fans and jewelry. as the show progresses.

THE DIVINE RISING STAR

By Robert W. Cabell

SCENE I

FROM BIRTH TO BORDELLO

(We hear the sound of wind chimes as a ghostly blue light rises on a woman's face as if hovering in the air. French phrases are spoken.)

SARAH
    For me there is no heaven except inside the hallowed halls of a theater. I am Madame Sarah Bernhardt. In my time, I was the greatest actress in the world, a time long forgotten by most of you.
(Wind chimes sound again as the lights warm and widen to show a lithe woman with long flowing red hair in in a diaphanous gown of white.)
    So—I have returned to my old "haunts" as the English say.
(Wind chimes once more as she opens her arms wide to indicate the stage.)
    Reincarnated in the mystical place where imagination is the truest form of reality.
(The lights warm to a normal tone and she seems to solidify.)
    From Montreal to Mombasa, I traveled throughout the world playing all the great classics in all the great theaters, and always in French. Yes, I am speaking to you in English. I swore I would die before I performed in any language but French. And I did. *(Shrugs)* Dying has a way of making one more accommodating. At seventy, I could still conjure the glamour of youth and play St. Joan of Arc. I would stand there with my eyes teary and defiant and

THE DIVINE RISING STAR –by Robert W. Cabell

SARAH
(Transforms her posture and movement into a youthful woman.)
cry. . . 'I am a maid of nineteen!' and the audience would cheer with acceptance! I loved being idolized. I do not know which was the greatest achievement—that they could accept me as nineteen... or as a virgin.
(Giggles and smiles seductively at the audience.)
The stories are true.
(She crosses to the side table with the decanter and pours herself a glass of wine as she speaks.)
Throughout the sixty-one years of my theatrical career, I did everything in my power to become famous and everything I needed to remain famous. But my life was not exactly heaven either. It was not filled with endless triumphs. There were many professional and personal failures.
(Smiles and shrugs.)
Quand même, in spite of everything, I was a great actress! My childhood was beyond my control. On October 25, 1844, I was born, how do you say, "at a very young age"...
(Smiles again.)
...to Youlie Van Hardt. Dutch by birth, she had a Jewish mother and a Catholic father, which seemed to become a pattern for the women of my family.
(She sets down her glass for a moment to take a kimono hanging on her dressing screen and slip into it. As she speaks.)
Mama left home at the age of fourteen and became a milliner by profession.
Utterly gorgeous, mama was swept off her feet,
(laughs slyly as she picks her wine glass back up and crosses back to the divan.)
literally, to Paris one day—imported by a Frenchman who wanted to conquer the world, one woman at a time.

SCENE I - FROM BIRTH TO BORDELLO

SARAH
(flounces down on to the divan.)
He was handsome, dashing, passionate, and quite unscrupulous! Once they arrived back in Paris, he promptly abandoned her.
(sips her wine.)
So, she found another milliner to work for until she found another man, Edouard Bernard, my father.
(She leans back on to the divan)
He, by the grace of God, was from a good Catholic family and not only recognized his paternity, but—his financial responsibilities.
(smiles.)
Mother never minded if a man loved and left her, as long as he left her enough.
(raises her glass as if in a toast, sips and sets the glass down.)
That resolved, Mama decided to apply her talents to a more profitable profession and became...a courtesan.
(shrugs and reclines back onto the divan)
Don't be shocked! The French admire a woman who can love a man for all he's worth. So—Mama brought her younger sister, Rosine, a lovely mercurial sylph, to Paris to share in her new "enterprise." Both were young and had the kind of beauty that made a man reach for his wallet.
(sits up and petulantly twirls her finger around a dangling curl)
I was an inconvenience so Mama judiciously shipped me off to Brittany with my father's old nurse and they both went on with their separate lives.
(gets up from the divan and crosses downstage left)
When I turned seven, at my Catholic father's insistence, I was sent to a convent school at Grand-Champs. There I formed a passionate attachment for Sister Marie-Odile.
(moves slowly across the stage from far left to far right)

THE DIVINE RISING STAR – by Robert W. Cabell

SARAH *(cont'd)*
She was the most wonderful person in the world. I could think of no string of pearls as lovely as her rosary beads, and no royal robes as elegant as the ebony barège veil that fell like a midnight shadow over the halo-white cambric that encircled her face. How I adored her. I wanted to be her! I became obsessed with being a nun.

After eight years at the school, which seemed on the one hand like a brief dream, and on the other a whole lifetime, my mother came and fetched me home. Home! I was going home! I was pleased and proud at long last, at age fifteen, to finally have a home.

SCENE II

THE CURTAIN RISES

SARAH
(gestures towards the divan)
My "home" was a demi-bordello inhabited by two well-dressed, languourous ladies—Mama and Aunt Rosine. Mama was living with the son of Napoleon's surgeon, Monsieur de Lancray—
(Sarah crosses to her dressing table and sits.
A man who had none of the virtues that I admired, and all of the vices I didn't.
During the next few lines she pulls her loose hair up upon her head. Ads some lip roug, earrings and blush to become more youthful and glamorous.)
Aunt Rosine's charms had garnered her no less than the Count de Mornay, the bastard half brother of Napoleon, and quite the diplomat. He could tell you to go to hell so tactfully; you'd be looking forward to the trip.
(Crosses stage left as she speaks)
By then I had two half sisters: the youngest one, Regina, and my middle sister Jeanne. During all those years away from Mama, I had nurtured the fantasy of a storybook mother. I had dreamed my mother cherished and adored me. In reality, only Jeanne elicited her maternal instincts. She had no such feelings for Regina or me.
(Crosses to down stage center)
It was Madame Guerard, the widow who lived on the floor above us, who would fulfill that role for me. One day, after a tirade of rants and raves, accomplishing nothing but making an utter fool of myself, I collapsed with my head in her lap and she promised to love and protect me so long as she lived. For the next forty years, that is precisely what my little lady did. It was from her that I learned that simple but absolutely extraordinary virtue, goodness.
(Crosses upstage center and flounces down on to the divan)

THE DIVINE RISING STAR –by Robert W. Cabell

SARAH
I was not beautiful like my sisters, or my glorious mother and aunt. I stuck out like a sore thumb in my mother's world of heavy velvet drapes, mirrored walls, and pine furniture. In a fateful moment one evening, the course of my life was suddenly set.
(Rises and stats to strut in a masculine manner.)
A notary from Le Havre arrived, and a family meeting was called concerning me. There in front of everyone, including Duc du Mornay, he informed my mother and me, that my father was hereby bequeathing me a hundred thousand francs.
(She "acts" out the story for each character)
'I don't want your money,' I said to the notary. 'I intend to dedicate my life to God! I shall become a nun and return to the convent.'
My mother sobbed in shock.
(changes her voice and demeanor to that of her mother)
"How can you say such awful things to me, Sarah?"
(rushes a few steps forward to the audience fling her arms wide.)
So I threw myself into my mother's arms, crying. I was crying from my eyelids, my hair, my fingers, my heart; my whole being was awash!
(Shrugs and puts her hands on her hips with a sigh of resignation.)
Mornay, who had paused to light a cigar, his face a mixture of boredom and puzzled amusement, remarked,
(In a dry masculine tone.)
"I have a feeling the child has a gift for the theater. Why don't you steer her in that direction?"
(back to herself.)

SCENE II - THE CURTAIN RISES

SARAH
And he walked out. Scarcely had he uttered those fateful words and departed, that I was dressed and climbing the steps of the Comédie-Française to see *Britannicus*.
(Whirls in childish delight.)
I had never attended a real play. I had no idea of what awaited me! The theater was swathed with men and women in their elegant best.

Gigantic crystal chandeliers blazing high above with prismatic shimmers vied for attention with glimmering gems and sparkling monocles below in a sea of plush, red velvet seats.
(In a hushed tone of awe.)
Suddenly the dizzying hum of voices subsided as waves of satin curtains rose on a set of stucco and false marble, and *Britannicus* entered. I was completely fixated, inundated with the beauty of Racine's verses, the actors, and overwhelmed with a divine certainty that this stage, this existence, was my destiny!

(In rueful masculine tone)
The hand of that destiny was the Duc de Mornay, who gained my entrance into the conservatory.

For everything in life there are 50,000 people who want to do the same thing as you and you must apply and excel in what you desire to achieve success. So I threw myself into my work, which consisted of two parts: on the one hand, I had to learn, understand, and remember the lines, and on the other, I had to try and ignore the advice of my professors!
(Mocking her past mentors)

THE DIVINE RISING STAR –by Robert W. Cabell

SARAH
This Monsieur wanted me to be natural, and that Monsieur wanted me to be sophisticated. Both claimed to be the definitive expert on the art of the theater, and neither of them ever agreed on anything!

(Smiles)
But in truth my dears, it doesn't really matter. Either you possess an innate and instinctive talent, or you don't.

At the end of each year came the competition and those who won went on to have professional careers. So I had to win! In my first year I won second prize and was determined to win first place the next year.
(She sits down at the edge of the divan with elegant posture and looks directly at the audience.)
I acted very radiantly, very effervescent and gay, and was warmly applauded. The accolades of the little crowd transformed me! I was certain I would win first prize. But first prize, by unanimous decision, was for my friend, Marie Lloyd.
(Mildly annoyed and slightly envious.)
Marie was a very tall beauty with a timorous charm and her long, flexible swan-like neck supported her beautiful, oval face. The costume she chose to wear didn't show a lot of style, but it showed a lot of woman. It was a prize for beauty that Marie Lloyd won! My second prize was for my acting.

That was my first artistic epiphany! I have never forgotten Marie's prize.

SCENE II - THE CURTAIN RISES

SARAH
So ever since, when I create a role, first I see the character in my imagination, in costume, with hair styled, walking, greeting, sitting, and standing. I imbue my body with this mental picture from which the soul must emerge.

When I did *Cleopatra's* death scene...
(She gives a sultry laugh.)
...I did it with live snakes entwined around my arms,
(holds up her arms as if the snakes were sliding up around them.)
my little pets that I kept in a jewel box in my dressing room.

(She shifts into an extreme sensual mode as she rises from the divan and slinks forward to center stage.)

SARAH *(as CLEOPATRA)*

Give me my robe, put on my crown, I have immortal longings in me now no more. The juice of Egypt's grape shall moist this lip. Yare, yare, good Iris, quick. Methinks I hear Antony call. I see him rouse himself to praise my noble act. I hear him mock the luck of Caesar, which the Gods give men to excuse their after wrath. .

Husband, I come. Now to that name my courage proves my title! I am fire and air, my other elements I give to baser life. So, have you done? Come then and take the last warmth of my lips. .

(She brushes her fingers to her lips, then looks at her hand and smiles, and then releases the character and returns to being "Sarah".)

THE DIVINE RISING STAR –by Robert W. Cabell

SARAH
My dear friend, Mrs. Patrick Campbell, the leading actress of the English stage, once asked me why I bothered to dye even the palms of my hands with makeup, which the audience couldn't possibly see. 'Because, when I look at my hands,' I told her, 'I will not see my hands but the hands of the queen of Egypt!'

So, with my second prize victory two years in a row to validate me—and the considerable influence of the Duc du Mornay—I was offered a position with the Comédie - Française. Little Sarah was accepted into the inner sanctum of France's first theater, the House of Molier. Here was a stage! Vast—mysterious—with its ramparts denuded of sets. The stage was eerie in its barrenness and the darkened theater sent shivers through my body.

The role of Iphigenia was my debut. I spent most of that afternoon on the Rue Duphot looking at the theater posters, my eyes glued to the one advertising the "First Performance of Mademoiselle Sarah Bernhardt". At 5:00 p.m. when I walked into the theater, my knees were shaking so much I was staggering like a drunkard!

I was nearly hysterical with fear and immobilized by doubt when the callboy shouted the curtain was about to go up. My arms were made of lead, my feet mortared to the floor, and my teeth chattered like castanets. There I was, standing on this Roman set with painted columns and painted facades, with artificial lights and painted faces—this was my new world.
(She takes a beat and looks at the audience for a moment before she continues.)

SCENE II - THE CURTAIN RISES

SARAH
Throughout my career I was plagued by horrific paralyzing fits of stage fright. The more important the role, the more severe the seizure. That night, my whole career seemed laid out for me. To my young mind it didn't seem possible that my life should follow such a steady path—and of course it didn't.
(She crosses to table and picks up her glass of wine to take a sip and carries it with her for a while.)
Disaster was lurking a few months away on the celebration of Moliere's birthday. The great one's day was always marked by a gala evening at the theater with the entire company gathering before his bust to pay him homage. It was the first time I would play a part in this ceremony and my youngest sister, Regina, begged to come. I adored her, so I acquiesced.
(glares at the audience.)
The disaster came in the unfortunate portly form of Madame Nathalie. That night I would learn the old sow deserved her reputation for a foul mouthed, foul tempered, vicious gossip.
(Stomps her foot and puts the glass of wine down and takes a moment to collect herself.)
We arrived as everyone was hurrying down the hallway. We were all crowed together and little Regina accidentally stepped on the train of Madame Nathalie's dress.
(puts her hands on her hips and then gesticulates as she speaks.)
That old hippopotamus turned and shoved Regina so hard, she fell and struck her face against one of the columns and it erupted in blood. I was livid! 'You hideous whore!' I cried, and I slapped her soundly across the face and rushed to my sister's side as the dreadful old cretin fainted on the spot.

THE DIVINE RISING STAR –by Robert W. Cabell

SARAH
The following day, Monsieur Thierry, the director of the theater, demanded that I publicly apologize to Madame Nathalie. I refused. I was expelled. It was 1862. I was eighteen years old.

Quand même... in spite of everything, I would become a great actress! I did not care. I kept acting, performing in a few shows at Gymnase Theater, which is how I met and fell madly in love with Prince Henri de Ligne of Belgium. Henri was to father the only true and constant love of my life, my son Maurice, born December 22, 1864.

I had been one of the actresses from the Gymnase invited to perform before the Emperor at the Tuileries, for which I innocently chose two Victor Hugo poems to recite. They where passionate and quite charming in their verse, and not being politically minded at the age of nineteen, I was unaware—or forgot, or simply suffered from a lapse of sanity when I chose them.

You see, Victor Hugo was in a self-imposed exile for his adverse and vehement protests against imperialism and this self-same Emperor, Napoleon III. So my choice was a "faux pas" in the extreme! The Emperor and Empress stood up and left during my performance. The stage manager grabbed me by the arm and hurled obscenities at me until I was in tears. It was then that the gallant Prince Henri came to my rescue and told them to stop yelling at me and leave me alone.

SCENE II - THE CURTAIN RISES

SARAH
> However, a year later, after a long, passionate affair, when I sadly informed Henri that I was pregnant with his child, the gallantry was gone.
>
> He looked at me with a toss of his regal brow and retorted, "Madame, when one sits on a bunch of thorns, how can one be sure which thorn has pricked her?" Mon dieu! There was only one "prick"—and he was it!
>
> Needless to say the affair was over and he neither recognized his son nor supported him. A Prince Charming, yes; a knight in shining armor, no. It was 1865. I was then twenty and a single mother.
>
> Quand même! In spite of everything, I still wanted to become a great actress! So, in 1866 I took my first true steps in that direction when I joined the Odeon Theater.

SCENE III

THE ODEON YEARS

SARAH
(Sarah glows with pleasant memories.)
    The Odeon is the one theater I truly loved and left with great regret. We were true friends, all young and jolly. Duquesnel was tall and gallant and a director of great charm and wit.
(her happy smiles changes to one of tolerance)
    His partner Chilly was the business manager of the theater. He always tried to make every dollar go as far as possible, and every girl too. *(Shrugs)* At the Odeon it was talent that mattered. There was none of the rigid détente, vicious gossip, or paranoid jealousy I had suffered through at the Comédie-Française, or the vapid frivolity of the Gymnase. At the Odeon, we lived and breathed our art.

    One day Mama came to see me rehearse in the theater, which she found horribly dark and dank. "You unlucky child," she cried, "how can you survive in here?"
(Laughs.)
    I not only survived, I thrived! To me it was like a great, dark factory in which as joyous jewelers of our art, we cut the precious stones furnished us by the poets.

    My first real taste of stardom, and the cementing of a life long friendship with Mademoiselle Agar, was in a piece called *Le Passant*, a one act play in verse, written in her honor by Francois Coppee. Agar played the role of Silvia, the Venetian courtesan, who grew weary and longed for the return of sweet, untainted love and moonlit gardens where hope springs eternal. I played the role of Zanetto, an idealistic young balladeer.

SCENE III - THE ODEON YEARS

SARAH *(as ZANETTO)*

My humor is my guide, I travel light and free as does an autumn leaf, as do the clouds that flee. I am brother of things that only seem and come of parts unknown. The poet born to dream, Who yearns for nothing but for freedom light and space. And as a flight of birds, will pass without a trace I stay not long enough to give a song anew, but linger in the woods to cull in morning dew the flowers sweet that deck this instrument of mine. I am the traveler you hardly can define, the youthful passerby for whom life is a play and, in the night, would seem a glowworm on the way. . .

SARAH
It was a petite and perfect little masterpiece.
(takes a moment)
My career had finally taken flight—when it was rudely interrupted—by WAR! How vehemently I hated the infinite grief it caused. When war with Germany was announced, I sent my family off to Le Havre to stay with cousins of my paternal grandmother. I returned to Paris with my little lady, Madame Guerard, to do whatever I could to save my beloved city from what you now call the Franco-Prussian War. We turned the Odeon Theater into a hospital.

We needed supplies. My little lady and I went to the office of the prefect prepared to beg for them. Imagine my total delight when the young prefect turned out to be none other

THE DIVINE RISING STAR –by Robert W. Cabell

SARAH *(cont'd)*
than Keratry, a gallant young officer in whose arms and bed I had lost my virginity. We'd had a marvelous affair until he was re-stationed in Mexico, and I had not seen him for several years. He was so pleased with my intentions that he gave me ten barrels of red wine, two of brandy, thirty thousand eggs, a hundred bags of coffee, twenty boxes of tea, forty cases of biscuits, and a thousand boxes of preserves.

Voila! We were, as you say, "in business!" I was transformed with delight. Then I saw his fur overcoat lying across an armchair. It would keep one of the wounded warm.

'Keratry, Cherie! A new fur coat would do a lot for me, and I would do a lot for a new fur coat.' He laughed and asked my permission to keep a lovely white silk scarf that was in the pocket. It was very pretty, but I relented and let him keep it.

The enemy army held Paris in a suffocating embrace that tightened every day, made worse by the fact that it was one of the coldest winters in history, and coal and wood were extremely scarce. The sick and wounded needed heat and I did the inconceivable; I burned all the little seats, the wooden property crates, benches, and armchairs, in the theater.

She shudders with the memory of the cold and covers herself with a heavy dark velvet cloak.

SCENE III - THE ODEON YEARS

SARAH
On December 27, 1870, the bombardment of Paris began. Every night we heard the lugubrious cry of "Ambulance! Ambulance!" as a sad procession of carriages full of wounded soldiers arrived. The men were stretched out on beds of blood stained straw as bombs exploded like fireworks, illuminating the sky with their terrifying beauty, then fragmented, raining death and destruction.

One day when my surgeon, Baron Larrey, came to see a patient who was very ill, he needed a prescription which his young apprentice, Victor, was instructed to retrieve at once from the small pharmacy on the corner. He was an adorable little scamp whom I called Toto. He had only gone a few meters when I clapped my hands and shouted, 'Come back!' as he was split open by a shell as it struck the child full in the chest and exploded. His poor entrails were spilled on the ground and his angelic little face was rendered of all its skin. A face sans eyes, sans nose, sans everything but bloody strips of fabric and bones. One more tragedy committed by the injustice and the infamy of war.

The bombardment of Paris continued. One night the Christian brothers came seeking hands and carriages to pick up the dead on the battlefield. I gave my two carriages and decided to go myself and help. Mon dieu, what an incredible Dantesque horror awaited me. An endless field of frozen, broken, bloody bodies. The first soldier I found alive had half his face...(*Shudders.*) ...clinging to life as he huddled against a mound of dead comrades for warmth. There were so many wounded that we could not carry them all. So many dead—so many dying.

THE DIVINE RISING STAR – by Robert W. Cabell

SARAH
When the Armistice was signed, Bismarck of Germany declared the price of peace for France was two hundred million francs—a sum that staggered even my grand imagination. Each Parisian felt the slap of the conqueror on his cheek. And I wanted my family! It was time for me to heal.

In time, the theaters of Paris opened their doors again and the Odeon decided to produce a new play, *Jean-Marie*, by Andre Theuriet. I played the role of a young woman imprisoned by an arranged marriage to an old man who subsisted through her memories of love. It was a moving and poetic part with a great sacrifice at the end that gave the role a touch of grandeur.

The war had cost us an Emperor but returned us our literary king, Victor Hugo, who would provide me with the crown of laurels that would finally make me a star.

It happened that same season in 1871 when they presented Hugo's *Ruy Blas*. Victor Hugo was a great genius. Witty, gallant, kind and refined, and his rehearsals were conducted with such grace and charm.

On January 26, 1872 the crème de la crème of Parisian society experienced a revelation, an artistic celebration at the premiere of this wonderful play.

I was starring in the role of the little queen. I played a German Princess married off to a Spanish King who ignored her and was always away from court, keeping her isolated and lonely.

SCENE III - THE ODEON YEARS

SARAH *(as the QUEEN)*

I think I shall be happier in my tomb. Never to watch the lingering sunset strew ruby and opal, like a laggard tide. Reluctant to retire, that heaps with gifts the gold strand of heaven. Nor hear again a wandering voice proclaim the reign of love, when evening in its cloak of darkness wraps the passion of the world. A phantom Queen that may not only look or listen, speak or think devoted daily to a living death. . .

SARAH
On that night, I suddenly found myself their "chosen one." I was surrounded by a sea of ardent admirers when, like the Red Sea, it parted before the great genius Hugo, who suddenly knelt before me! I trembled in awe of him as he took my hands, and pressing them to his lips cried, "Thank you, thank you!" Such powerful praise was beyond belief. I was totally undone!

I was twenty-seven and it was this great success that would sweep me forward to a new height in my career. I received a letter from Perrine, the manager of the Comédie-Française. He wanted me to rejoin their troupe. Don't think for one moment I was being disloyal or unappreciative of what those wonderful years at the Odeon had done for me. But one does not wear a lovely wool coat when a mink is handy.

THE DIVINE RISING STAR –by Robert W. Cabell

SARAH

There was no more prestigious theater in all of Europe than the Comédie-Française. To refuse such an invitation would be a cataclysmic career mistake, not to mention the fact they were offering me much more money.

Victor Hugo gave a lovely party to celebrate the 100th performance of *Ruy Blas*. Chilly was still angry with me for my impending move to the Comédie -Française the next season, but we had a fragile truce for the evening.

We were seated side by side at the table when he collapsed onto his plate in the middle of making a remark. 'Chilly, don't be vulgar,' I said. 'The joke isn't very funny!' Alas, it was no joke and poor Chilly was, as you say, "dead as a doorknob."

I was utterly astonished. People died in beds, or hospitals, not cutoff mid-sentence at a soiree! Death had no place there. Pomp and circumstance and comedy were shields against it—or so I had always thought. But death knows no restrictions.

The Reaper also coveted my dear sister Regina. She had the palest blond hair I had ever seen, the beauty of a Madonna, and the mouth of a dockworker. During the last few months of her life, I slept in the same room with her to take care of her every need, but nothing could save her. By the tender age of eighteen, Regina rushed into Death's arms from tuberculosis, exacerbated through endless rounds of debauchery and drugs. She had lived her life with a vengeance.

SCENE III - THE ODEON YEARS

SARAH
>Drugs seemed to unleash a deep-rooted streak of violence and a craving for sensationalism. This was true for my other sister Jeanne, who also died in her early thirties, and my husband Damala, twelve years my junior who would die at thirty-four. I desperately wanted them all to live, but they all did their best to die.

ଔଆଔଆଔଆଔଆଔଆ

SCENE IV

THE COMÉDIE –FRANÇAISE

SARAH

At the Comédie-Française, I achieved great success once again in a Victor Hugo play *Hermani* in the role of Doña Sol. To play the title role, and my leading man, they cast Mounet Sully. He was the most famous actor of the day, an Adonis who incarnated the twin virtues of professionalism and virility and was somehow also childishly beguiling. We fell madly in love.

Unfortunately, Mounet Sully was also dumb as a stump. And I was used to men of substance such as Keratry and Charles Haas, not some poor boy who was paid exactly the same salary I was.

Sex is the thing that takes the least amount of time and causes the most amount of trouble. One day Mounet discovered I had gone to bed with another man. He was livid and shouted in front of the entire company, "You slept with that man!"

'Not a wink,' I protested.

To make matters worse, I was playing Desdemona to his Othello. I was terrified! When in the final scene Othello hurls Desdemona onto the bed to smother her, I panicked. I squealed like a stuck pig, "Don't touch me! I have done nothing! I am innocent! Someone help me!"

I had no intention of sacrificing myself to my art, and due to the scenes that had taken place backstage, the stage manager brought down the curtain, ending the scene and saving my life!

SCENE IV - THE COMÉDIE-FRANÇAISE

SARAH
Though the Comédie-Française was the most prestigious, it was not the most convivial theater to work in. Perrine, the manager of the Comédie and I were constantly at odds. I owed everything I had to him. Ulcers, headaches, nausea...

I spent as little time at the theater and rehearsals as possible and took up painting and sculpting, having several shows and quite a bit of success. In addition to my art, in 1878, at thirty-four, I fell passionately in love with ballooning. Every day, I went up in Monsieur Giffard's tethered balloon at the Tuilleries. This persistency had struck the savant, and I said, 'How I should like to go up in a balloon that is not captive.'

"Well, mademoiselle, you shall do so if you like," he replied, very kindly.

'When?' I asked.

"Any day you wish."

So, we made arrangements, and on the appointed day,

George Clairin, Young Godard, and I arrived at dawn to see rise up before us a plump, soft, mushroom-shaped object, which seemed to spring from the earth. As we watched, it completely inflated and lurched skyward against its moorings.

THE DIVINE RISING STAR –by Robert W. Cabell

SARAH
> M. Giffard waved us all aboard and we ascended into the clouds in the *Doña Sol*. She was a beautiful orange-colored balloon named in honor of my acclaimed portrayal of that Victor Hugo heroine.
>
> The rumor of our flight was soon out but too late for the press to catch us. Suddenly Perrine arrived, howling with disbelief as we soared off into the sky. I was enraptured up in the clouds surrounded by my friends, sipping champagne as we nibbled on sandwiches of goose paté.
>
> Paris lay beneath us in a glorious gilt of sunlight while a turquoise sky with soft diaphanous clouds passed by us with spectral caresses. And everywhere was silence—such velvety silence.
>
> Then suddenly a thrum began to intrude upon our ears when a flock of larks engulfed the balloon as they hurtled by. It was glorious! Overwhelmingly glorious!
>
> With the approach of twilight, the air became charged
>
> with poetry as we descended in unison with the sun, touching the earth just as it slipped, fiery red, beneath the horizon.
>
> When I returned home late that night, there was a letter waiting from Perrine. He was a very kind man, but not the good kind. He listing my caprices, eccentricities, and announcing that I was to be fined one thousand francs for making my aerial escapade without his permission. I went to see him just to laugh in his face!

SCENE IV - THE COMÉDIE-FRANÇAISE

SARAH

'How dare you fine me! As long as I fulfill my engagements, I do as I please with my life, you little troglodyte!' And I promptly resigned.

The Minister of Fine Arts was not happy. The next day when they assured me that M. Perrine had over-stepped his authority, they asked that I withdraw my resignation, which I did. Someday he would go too far—and I hoped he stayed there.

It was all too strained a situation to continue working under, so it was not surprising that the visit of the Comédie-Française to London caused the final rupture. An American impresario named Edward Jarrett, known as the Bismarck of managers, came to see me in Paris before our departure for London.

He was a handsome man, with straight, serious features, who stood there and offered me outrageous amounts of money to perform privately in English drawing rooms after the theater. It was to be the beginning of a beautiful friendship.

SCENE V

THE ACCOLADES OF LONDON

SARAH

I loved London as much if not more than it loved me. I am quite an Anglophile! It is the only capital in the world where society—high society—is also endowed with imagination.

In London one can meet and socialize with the Prince of Wales, who purchased several of my paintings, and his lovely Princess Alexandria, with whom I became dear friends. And the likes of Lord and Lady Dudley, Lady Cumberman, and the Duke of Albany, as well as Ellen Terry, Mrs. Patrick Campbell, and my dear Oscar Wilde—with all the élan and bon vivant you'd find amongst the intellects and artists of Paris.

London put the gilded edge to my French reputation and made it international.

It was on the second of June, 1879 at the Gaiety Theatre, that I met London across the footlights for the very first time. I was to perform the second act of *Phaedra* by Rancine, a play whose title character was driven by terrible passions imposed upon her by Venus, the goddess of love. Married to Thesius, king of Athens, she was condemned to desperate love for her stepson, Hippolytus, son of Thesius and the queen of the Amazons.

But there was no Act One to build the character. I was terrified! Three times I had applied my makeup, and three times I had taken it off. I felt I looked too thin, too short, and ugly in my costume.

SCENE V - THE ACCOLADES OF LONDON

SARAH
There was no time to change and nowhere to retreat. I grew hysterical at what I thought would be my theatrical demise. I threw myself onto the stage like an angry sacrifice!

SARAH *(as PHAEDRA)*
I, jealous! And it's with Theseus I would plead! My husband lives, and still my passions feed. On whom? Toward whom do all my wishes tend? At every work, my hair stands up on end, the measure of my crimes is now replete. I foul the air with incest and deceit. My murderous hands are itching to be stained with innocent blood, that vengeance be obtained. Wretch that I am, how can I live, how face the sacred sun, great elder of my race?.

My grandsire was, of all the Gods, most high; my forebears fill the world, and all the sky. Where can I hide? For Hades' night I yearn. No, there my father holds the dreadful urn entrusted to his hands by Fate, it's said: there Minos judges all the ashen dead. Ah, how his shade will tremble with surprise to see his daughter brought before his eyes forced to confess a throng of sins, to tell of crimes perhaps unheard of yet in Hell..

THE DIVINE RISING STAR - *by Robert W. Cabell*

SARAH
London adored me. Oscar Wilde dubbed me "The Divine," and the entire city began calling me "The Divine Sarah Bernhardt!" And the money I was making through my bookings with Jarrett was three times what I made through the Comédie-Française!

One week after I concluded my performance, I decided to train down to Liverpool and buy some lion cubs from a menagerie owned by a Mr. Cross.

I love big cats, anything jungle-ish. I even consulted numerous physicians about grafting a tiger's tail to my buttocks. It would have made for marvelous entrances and exits—but none could assist me.

Aside from that, this Mr. Cross had such fantastic creatures! But the only things youthful enough to suit me were a juvenile cheetah, which was very pensive and sulked sadly in his little cage, and a lovely white wolf, fanged and fiery-eyed. He looked terrifying but was really a lamb.

Mr. Cross decided to gift me with a tiny herd of six chameleons, a dainty breed of lizards, along with a larger specimen that looked fabulously prehistoric and changed colors. It went from pale green to dark bronze. I was so delighted with it, I had a local jeweler create a tiny gold collar and chain for it, so I could pin the chain to my shoulder and let it run around flashing colors like a living Jurassic corsage! I called it Cross-chi Cross-ca in honor of Mr. Cross.

SCENE V - THE ACCOLADES OF LONDON

SARAH
    We returned to London with the cheetah in a cage, the wolf on a leash, my six little chameleons in a box, and Cross-ci Cross-ca on my shoulder. I introduced them to my other little group of fauna—my three dogs, my parrot, Bizibouzou, and my monkey, Darwin.

    My little lady was not thrilled with the new collection, and my butler was afraid of the wolf as we all gathered in the garden. I insisted the cheetah be released from his cage, and he burst forth overjoyed with freedom.

    As he raced for a tree, the dogs began to howl with terror, the parrot shrieked strident cries of panic, the monkey screeched and shook his cage, and my wolf growled and gnashed his dagger-like fangs!

    All the windows of the surrounding apartments immediately flew open, startled by the furious calliope of animal cries. When a crowd of faces appeared above my garden wall, I was seized with a fit of uncontrollable laughter, while my friend George Clairin, shaking in amusement, sketched the never-to-be-forgotten scene.

    The London papers were bursting with headlines the following day, all pontificating about the bazaar bedlam that had been loosed upon 77 Chester Square.

    The Comédie-Française gave its last London performance on July 12, and we returned to Paris. I had resolved to submit my resignation.

THE DIVINE RISING STAR - *by Robert W. Cabell*

SARAH
>The jealousies and deliberate slights and exasperations inflicted on me by Perrine were no longer tolerable. He was forcing me to perform Clorinde in *L'Aventurière*, a role I detested, in a play I despised, as punitive retribution for my personal success in London.
>
>Both the production and I were a miserable failure. I submitted my resignation thereafter. I had only completed five years of my twenty-year contract, and they fined me 100,000 francs. But I was free.

෴෴෴෴෴

SCENE VI

THE FRENCH INVASION OF AMERICA

SARAH

It was 1880, I was just thirty-six, and on my own. Once more Edward Jarrett entered my life as the Pied Piper that lured me, and my troupe, to America. He spun golden dreams, which he largely fulfilled, and sometimes surpassed. After a substantial advance and weeks of construction, I loaded my own sets, costumes, and company on a vessel appropriately named the *Amérique* and sailed for New York.

But it was so hard to leave my son. As a child, Maurice likened me to a bird. His "little mamma bird," he would say, for I would spread my wings and soar off to faraway places without a moment's notice, leaving him alone with his nanny. But I always returned with an armful of presents and a heart full of kisses, so he forgave me. Unfortunately, it set up a pattern that lasted until I died.
On the day of his birth, I held him for the first few beats of his heart. On the day of my death, he held me for the last few beats of mine. Quand même, in spite of everything, we adored each other.

So—on to New York. I invited my little lady to accompany me along with my sister Jeanne. But, a few days before we departed, my sister, a morphine addict, suffered from an overdose and had to convalesce in a sanitarium for several weeks. For that reason, we agreed that she would rest and then join the tour in America. I looked high and low for a replacement, but I didn't look low enough before I engaged Marie Colombier, whom I had considered a friend for twenty years, to play the roles

THE DIVINE RISING STAR - *by Robert W. Cabell*

SARAH

Jeanne normally played. Like the viper Cleopatra held to her breast, she bore nothing but poison to me. One casting choice I made that I did not regret was my leading man, Eduardo Angelo. He was extremely handsome, hard as a rock, stroke-able as a rabbit, and performed the role of my leading man on and off stage throughout the tour.

One evening, several days out of port, it had turned cold and the sea was tossing the ship about. I was not encumbered by seasickness, and having a great love for boats of all kinds, I felt the need for fresh air, so I decided to stroll about the deck. I saw a very somber woman dressed in black and nodded a silent greeting to her as we passed.

But just at that moment a sudden swell sent the boat pitching drastically to one side. I lurched forward and clutched the railing. I saw the other lady hurtling toward the open stairwell, and I frantically grabbed a handful of her dress and kept her from falling headfirst down the steep and narrow stairwell.

'Are you all right, Madame? Mon dieu, you could have been killed!'

"Yes, I might have," she said, tinged with regret. "But it was not God's will."

Then she looked at me with huge soulful eyes that seemed to focus from far away to the present. "Thank you, Madame," she said. "Do I know you?"

SCENE VI - THE FRENCH INVASION OF AMERICA

SARAH
'Perhaps,' I replied, 'I am Sarah Bernhardt.' She drew back as if from a leper.

"The actress? Oh my!" She straightened her little body with a sudden regal grace and said, "I am Mary Todd Lincoln, the President's widow."

I gasped softly as she nodded and walked away. I had just saved the life of a woman whose husband had been assassinated by another actor.

I went straight to my cabin and remained there for two days. I was terrified of meeting this woman again for whom I had such deep respect and sympathy, but to whom I should never have had the effrontery to speak.

We were all restless and anxious to make port on the morning of October 27, 1880. When I looked out my porthole, I saw two ships sailing toward us. One was packed with journalists and officials, the other with an orchestra playing "La Marseillaise."

Ever the actress, I stood tall, wrapped my furs around me, and with a regal toss of my head, turned to the mob of photographers and reporters that suddenly swarmed the ship, assailing me with a barrage of questions.

THE DIVINE RISING STAR - *by Robert W. Cabell*

SARAH

One exceedingly obnoxious fellow had the audacity to ask me if it was true that I had four children by four different men who I had never married.

'Of course not,' I replied. 'But even that wouldn't be as bad as American women I've heard of who have married four different husbands and had no children by any of them!'

Several photographers kept shouting, "We want a picture of you in your coffin!" Merd! Would they never stop bothering me about that?!

Throughout my career, the papers were always full of lurid rumors that I was a necrophile. This, no doubt, was due to the fact that I kept an open coffin in my bedroom.

You see I was ill at fifteen, and told I would soon die. To pick my own place of eternal rest was in fact comforting to me. It was really quite lovely, made of rosewood and elegantly lined with white satin, which I replaced religiously every two years when it began to fade and yellow. The upholstery fees alone where enough to give one a heart attack. But, it cupped my hips and encircled my shoulders like a satin glove—a haven where I went when I was in desperate need of solitude.

After a few disparaging inquires about my coffin, the entire scene became too aggressive and uncontrollable. I knew better than to look to Jarrett to curtail the interviews, so I merely fluttered my eyes and collapsed into his strong arms.

SCENE VI - THE FRENCH INVASION OF AMERICA

SARAH

My little lady came forth to defend me and insisted that I be taken to my hotel so I could recover in peace. That was my first entrance into the New York theatrical world. I loved New York. I found it a very exciting and masculine city. The Brooklyn Bridge, so long and strong! How did they ever erect it? I found the streets of Manhattan were totally safe; it was the people you had to watch out for—like those truly odious people from customs. As New York was our first port of call, all my costumes and sets had to be inspected and valued for duty and customs taxes. I arrived at the theater on my second day to find my forty-two trunks stacked together in the center of the stage, with twenty-one men, each positioned in between two trunks.

A man strode forward with an odiferous stump of a cigar wedged in the corner of his mouth. He was a real character, which in French means a jerk with personality. He garbled something at me that was impossible to comprehend in any language and signaled forty hands to rummage through my wardrobe! Two hundred soiled fingers, with dirty, grimy fingernails, were riffling through my delicate silks and satins and velvet dresses!

I shrieked! I howled! I sprang like an enraged tiger upon the stage to save my glorious costumes from this filthy violation as I backed the startled platoon of goons against a wall. I insisted that only my wardrobe mistress, and my maid, remove each dress for their inspection. Just at that moment, two horrific, loathsome creatures that were presented to me as women waddled forward.

THE DIVINE RISING STAR - *by Robert W. Cabell*

SARAH
    The first was as thick as she was wide and had a nose that obstructed the rest of her face from view, except unfortunately her muzzle-like mouth. The other was gaunt and withered, with a hunch to her back and a wag to her head that made her look like a turtle.

    They were evidently dressmakers hired by customs to assess the value of the costumes. "They're gorgeous!" they shrieked. "How exquisite!" they howled. "Such luxuriant fabrics!" they hissed.

    It took a total of three days for the cow and the turtle to finish their evaluation, which ended in costing the exorbitant sum of twenty-eight thousand francs!

    On Monday, November 8, at eight thirty, the curtain went up for my first New York performance. I had chosen *Adrienne Lecouvreur* for my debut.

She sits at her makeup table as she continues to speak and touches up her makeup and styles her hair as she speaks and changes here jewels for the new role.
    Adrienne was the mistress of Maurice de Saxe, who was also the lover of the Princess de Bouillon, a married woman whose husband was the Prince Royal. The drama ended with my assassination as I was poisoned by my rival—the adulterous Princess.

She rises from her makeup table and crosses stage left to the footlights as the stage lights dim and a spot light rises behind the footlights..

SCENE VI - THE FRENCH INVASION OF AMERICA

SARAH
> The theater was, how you say, "jam-packed." The audience waited impatiently for my entrance. They came expecting to be shocked and instead became fascinated and seduced by a nymph across the footlights.

(SARAH as) **ADRIENNE**
> My chest is burning! It's like a fire, like a devouring fire that is consuming me. Ah—the pain increases—Maurice—you, who love me so, save me! Succor me. I do not wish to die! .A little while ago I could have implored to die as happiness—I was so unhappy—but now I do not wish to die. Michonnet! Maurice loves me! He has called me his wife! My God release me! Let me live a few days yet—a few days near him. I am so young, and life appears to me now, so beautiful I feel the power of existence is escaping me. Do not leave me Maurice! Very soon my eyes will see you no longer, and my hand will not be able to press yours.

She dies and the lights fade down and out, then rise as the audience applauds SARAH rises and crosses downstage center

SARAH
> For America I had picked a repertoire of eight plays, in all but one of which I died nightly in various noble or ignoble manners. I died by poison. I died of a broken heart.

THE DIVINE RISING STAR - by Robert W. Cabell

SARAH
    I expired from old age, suicide, and murder—dying gracefully, willingly, humiliated, or martyred. I died a thousand deaths across the nation. Fifty-two cities in America could soon claim, "Sarah Bernhardt died here!"
She sits and removes her jewelry, softens her hair and makeup and slips into a filmy bed-jacket as she speaks.
    It was in America not France, that I gave my very first performance as Marguerite in *La Dame aux Camélias*, on November 16, 1880, at New York's Booth Theater.
    It was the first of over 3,000 performances of what was to be my greatest role.
SARAH crosses to the Divan and lies down as she speaks wile the stage goes dim and a pool of light envelopes her.

(SARAH as) **MARGUERITE**

    I am dying, but I am so happy, and my joy conceals my death. Armand, give me your hand. I assure you that it's not difficult to die. How strange it all is.
(She struggles to rise.)
    I'm not suffering any more. It seems as though life were pouring into me. I feel so well. I never felt so well before. I am going to live! Oh, how well I feel.
(She dies.)

She hold a few beats of silence then laughs and sits up with a look of delight as she addresses the audience.

SCENE VI - THE FRENCH INVASION OF AMERICA

SARAH
It was such a success, that my repertoire was changed so that if I should give only one performance in any city, it would be *La Dame aux Camélias*.
She rises and crosses to her dressing screen, slipping off the bed jacket and drapes it on the screen.
Why Americans always insist on calling the show "Camille" has never ceased to amaze me. There is no such character in the play.
Sara slips into a pair of long lacey gloves and then picks up a lace trimmed parasol as she crosses downstage center
If I gave a second performance, it would be the role of Gilbert in *Frou-frou*, the only frivolous character I portrayed in my repertoire.

(SARAH as) **GILBERT**

I admit that he is a man to whom it is next to impossible to say "no." What did they tell me he might become? Oh yes—a minister or an ambassador—and I am an ambassadress! How I should like to be one, IF, I could be one in Paris!
Sarah pops open her parasol and saunters thoughtful for a moment.
But I am full of bad qualities, little sister, you know it and so do I, and it appears to me that these are the very things M. de Sartorys ought to wish his wife possessed of if he desires to be downright unhappy.

THE DIVINE RISING STAR - *by Robert W. Cabell*

GILBERT *(Cont'd)*

He will correct them? I am not sure he will. I have always been spoiled, first by Papa and then by you! What is especially disquieting is that I am resolved not to allow myself to be corrected of those lovely faults, as I happen to be perfectly content with my little self. The conflict between him and me will be more serious than you imagine. He is a very strong man. I know, but –were he a hundred fold stronger, were he strong enough to rule Europe, I should not consider it proven that he was strong enough to direct Frou-frou!

As she finishes the speech Sarah closes the parasol and tamps the ground with it, as if she was stomping her foot.

SARAH

(Laughs) Yes, little Frou-frou enjoyed being spoiled, and so did I. I was totally spoiled by my "Palace Train Car" that Jarrett and Mr. Henry Abbey, my American director, had created for me. Such luxury! The dernier cri, the ultimate in travel luxury. Paneled walls of lustrous, inlaid woods, burnished brass lamps, potted plants, paintings, Persian carpets, and fur rugs all lit with jewel colors from the stained glass insets above every door and window. A dining room for ten, a bedroom with a brass bed big enough for Angelo and me to practice all my love scenes, and a little basket bed for my dog, Hamlet.

SCENE VI - THE FRENCH INVASION OF AMERICA

SARAH
My favorite spot was at the end of the car on my little observation platform, furnished with comfortable wicker chairs, where I spent many blissful hours with my little lady, watching the magnificent landscapes approach and then flash by. Such sunsets and moonrises—it was exhilaratingly beautiful scenery. The evening we left for Boston. Mr. Jarrett and Mr. Abbey made arrangements for us to stop at Menlo Park to call on Thomas Edison, and there before us, a field of stars had descended, strung like garlands along the lane and through the trees. The miraculous, lighted globes of Mr. Edison were astonishingly beautiful!

My first question was, 'When will we ever have electricity in the theatre?' It seemed to, as you say, "break the ice." He spoke very little French, but I was especially charmed by his timid and courteous grace and by his profound love of Shakespeare, which seems to be the universal language of the theater. And Edison had the most marvelous blue eyes!—more luminous than his incandescent lamps. A half an hour later, we were the best of friends, and it was with great regret that I boarded my train and headed on to Boston.

Oh! Boston is the home of the most fabulous ladies in the world. They wear the most extraordinary hats and have the most charming good manners. And who could resist losing her heart to one of those adorable Harvard students who serenaded her? Most delightful of all was the chance to meet the genius poet, Henry Wadsworth Longfellow, whose work I absolutely adored!

THE DIVINE RISING STAR - *by Robert W. Cabell*

SARAH
(Laughs.)
   The old coot was seventy-three at the time—and was only willing to meet me if we had a chaperone!
(Smiles.)
   One's reputation can never be left at home.

   The only bad thing about Boston was Henry Smith, a repulsive, fast-talking entrepreneur who looked like a toad! He extended to me an invitation to visit a giant blue whale that he had captured and brought in still alive to the harbor. At "Mr. Toad's" insistence, I climbed up on to the poor creature's back.

   Thereafter I found myself followed from city to city by a huge poster inviting people to come view the since-dead whale. This whale was my Waterloo. Giant posters plastered each city claiming it had met its demise at the hand of none other than Sarah Bernhardt, merely for the sake of procuring whalebone for my corset!

   I do not now, nor did I ever wear a corset, a fact of my life that was totally lost on the public. I would have given anything to cut that odious fellow, Smith, up into little pieces and feed him to Moby Dick!

   When I arrived in your "Windy City," Chicago, it was like a scene right out of *Andrienne Lecouvreur*! Just as in the scene where she meets her lover to be, Maurice, I was also saved that day, though instead of a drunken crowd of amorous soldiers, it was a mass of admirers.

SCENE VI - THE FRENCH INVASION OF AMERICA

SARAH
> I was mobbed at the train station and nearly trampled to death by adoring fans. A woman came at my face jabbing at me with a pair of scissors to clip a lock of my
>
> hair. Another attacked the hem of my dress. Someone tore my hat from my head and a piranha-like school of fans ripped it apart as the rest snatched and clutched at my fur wrap.
>
> I screamed! Two huge hands encircled my waste and hoisted me off my feet and into the air. This was the end! But no, I landed on the shoulders of some Goliath. He forced his way through the crowd and deposited me in the nearest cab that raced me to my hotel.
>
> The next morning I saw in the headlines that this man, my gallant savior, was an escaped prisoner convicted of killing his lover and condemned to die. He had been recaptured—due to his kindness to me! I could not believe this. How could someone so kind and courageous be a cold-blooded killer? I went to the prison immediately with my company in tow to see him and perform for the inmates. I was horrified to find he was to be hanged the next day. He swore with his last breath he was innocent, and I believed him.
>
> In St. Louis, Jarrett and Abbey hatched another one of their publicity schemes using my jewelry as, how do you say, "an angle." They presented a jeweler to me who offered to clean and repair all my pieces for free.

THE DIVINE RISING STAR - *by Robert W. Cabell*

SARAH

In return he merely wished to exhibit them in his store for a few days. I was not enthusiastic about the plan, but the jeweler seemed pleasant and eagerly assured me that the exhibit would delight the local ladies, so I acquiesced.

He must have worked night and day, for within forty-eight hours, all my jewelry was in immaculate condition and dazzlingly displayed in his window. However, along with my real jewels, there were six pairs of earrings, two necklaces, sixteen bracelets, and thirty rings I had never laid eyes on in my life.

There was also a glorious lorgnette all in diamonds and rubies that I would gladly have claimed, and much to my dismay, a gold cigarette holder, even though I detested tobacco.

The papers valued my burgeoning collection at almost a million dollars, though a good portion of that was due to the erroneous additions! Inquiries from the local ladies came pouring in, and several pieces, none that were actually mine, were announced for sale. This was too much to bear. I tracked down M. Jarrett like a southern bloodhound and demanded he put an end to the charade.

On Sunday, January 30, 1881, I breathed a sigh of relief as we pulled out of the St. Louis station. I watched the city dwindle into the distance from my observation balcony. We had barely lost sight of the city when disaster struck. The conductor rushed toward me with alarm smeared across his brow and pleaded, "Madame, I beg you, go back inside your car!"

SCENE VI - THE FRENCH INVASION OF AMERICA

SARAH
>The moment I was inside, he pulled the alarm, motioned to another conductor, and they leapt off the train and dragged a man from underneath my private car. This man suddenly found himself surrounded by Jarrett, several conductors, and an armed guard that Jarrett and Abbey had hired. He quickly confessed to be a member of a gang planning to steal my jewelry. When Jarrett and his guard jammed a pistol against either side of his head, he poured out the details of their plot. The poor thug was securely tied hand and foot, and we immediately returned to St. Louis to hand him over to the authorities.
>
>Next, another train was sent ahead to spring a trap and apprehend the band of thieves. There was a fierce fight in which one of the thugs was killed, and two more wounded. The rest were taken prisoner.
>
>My jewelry and the deplorable abuse of publicity were the catalysts for all this and more. Days later, despite all my pleas, one of the culprits, Albert Wirtz, a twenty-five-year-old native of Belgium, was hung.
>
>I wept for him. I hated the death penalty! It was a vestige of cowardly barbarism. It was a disgrace for civilized countries still to be raising guillotines and gallows!
>
>Divine retribution was nearly the cost of our vanity. Our train ride to New Orleans almost ended all our lives—a ride that could have made me much guiltier than Albert Wirtz.

THE DIVINE RISING STAR - *by Robert W. Cabell*

SARAH
    You see the train was chugging along at its usual pace, when the brakes slammed to a stop. I looked out the window at this little station and saw the riverbanks swollen with water. Suddenly Jarrett leapt out, gesticulating wildly at the engineer. I clambered down the stairs of my little observation deck, furs, lace, and feathers flailing behind me, and raced over to join them.

    "The bridge is eroded by the flood and I cannot risk crossing the river," I heard the engineer yell at Jarret. In the same breath he informed me that there was no way to avoid similar situations in the area without back tracking halfway to Cincinnati.

    "Impossible!" screamed Jarret. "That will delay us at least two days, and we are sold out in New Orleans tonight!"

    No matter how Jarrett and I pleaded or demanded, he refused to budge, until the universal solvent of money dissolved the obstruction. The man was paid $2,500 dollars in advance, which was wired then and there from the train station to his wife, in case we did not make it.

    We boarded the train and told nothing to the troupe, except for my little "court." My little lady prayed, Jeanne rubbed her rabbit's foot, Angelo encircled a noble arm around my shoulder, and Marie nervously petted Hamlet. He bit her. Good doggie! That's why I love dogs. They wag their tails, not their tongues.

SCENE VI - THE FRENCH INVASION OF AMERICA

SARAH
We could feel the steam swelling inside the engine, bursting with pressure as we held our breath. We gasped as the train leapt suddenly forward at a cataclysmic speed hurtling across the bridge.

We were nearly across when a shudder swept through the train and the tracks began to moan as we lurched forward with a snap! The bridge had promptly collapsed behind us, as the last car cleared the banks.

I turned pale, wracked with guilt at my sheer gall. How could I have risked all those sweet lives?

The last indignity was yet to come. It was in Atlanta that God gave me, as you say, "the finger." I was bored and ready to finish the tour. I noticed from my little platform all these immense black crows in the trees and decided to have some sport. La! 'Stop the train!' I cried. 'Let's shoot some of these black messengers of Satin!'

Gypsies swear that crows are evil messengers, and I was in an evil mood. So, we started popping the little devils out of the sky. The local sheriff arrived a short time later and arrested the entire company, not for shooting crows—but for hunting on the Sabbath.

Well, after a day in jail, we boarded the train with our tails between our legs—and fled to New York!

THE DIVINE RISING STAR - *by Robert W. Cabell*

SARAH

By the time my weary troupe and I returned to New York—after surviving robberies, train wrecks, mob scenes, smelly dead whales, and incarceration—we had given one hundred fifty-seven performances in fifty-two cities.

We were glad to have gone to America, and even gladder to leave, as we boarded our ship. I had many fond memories, along with the $194,000 dollars profit, to take back with me as I waved good-bye to crowds of adoring fans and sailed back to France. France! Back to my adorable son, Maurice, who I had missed so madly.

〜〜〜〜〜

SCENE VII

RECONCILIATION

SARAH

I returned to Paris under a dark cloud of disapproval, created by Marie Colombier's vicious lies and slander she'd wired across the Atlantic. Unbeknownst to me, Marie had been serializing the tour through weekly cables to *L'Événement*. Her stories were, as you Americans love to say, "bitchy," exaggerated, and libelous—claiming that the tour and my performances were colossal failures.

Because of these lies, no manager came forward with an offer; no playwright submitted any script upon my return from one of the most successful theatrical tours in history! It was maddening. Even with the $194,000 American dollars I returned with, I lived an extravagant life with a little prince that spent like an emperor—but I needed to act!

At last, as you say, "opportunity knocked" in the form of a presidential gala at the opera, on the tenth anniversary of the armistice between Germany and France, in Paris on July 14, 1881.

The gala included performances by the greatest stars of the Comédie-Française, climaxing with a recitation of "La Marseillaise" by none other than my dear friend Mlle Agar.

Agar was still a beautiful woman prone to passionate affairs. It was easy to discover what hot-blooded young stallion was the current captain of her heart.

THE DIVINE RISING STAR - *by Robert W. Cabell*

SARAH
He was a rather dashing young officer, fortuitously stationed in Tours. Once more the Fates were kind, in that my dear friend Hortense was still Agar's dresser, and shared my mischievous sense of humor.

On the afternoon of the gala, the trap was sprung as Hortense rushed into Agar's garden, where she was resting before the performance. Scenes of anxiety and agitation had always been Hortense's forte, and she was now in her glory.

Tearfully, she related the grievous news she had received from the orderly of Agar's handsome captain. Apparently, he had fallen from his horse and was so badly injured, he had been taken to a hospital in Tours for surgery.

Sweet Agar embodied all the great love and self-sacrifice of the characters she portrayed. She leapt to her feet, called for her cloak, and rushed out the door to ride to the side of her beloved, instructing Hortense to find a replacement for her. Hortense gladly obliged.

It was an unsuspecting crowd of dignitaries and artistic giants that arrived at the gala that evening as Mounet Sully, still the reigning Adonis of the Parisian theater, neared the conclusion of his patriotic poem. The audience was charmed while the backstage was in panic. Mlle Agar had yet to arrive, and the time for her climactic performance was only moments away!

Sarah slips a hooded cloak around her shoulders and closes it with a clasp below her neck.

SCENE VII - RECONCILIATION

SARAH
>My theatrical sense of timing had always been instinctive and impeccable, and that night the sense of victory or death had honed it to perfection. I stepped in through the stage door as Mounet Sully arrived backstage with the applause from his performance still lingering.
>
>His eyes flew wide with astonishment, as did that of the stage-manger and the two directors. To Sully's credit, in spite of all that had passed between us, he dropped to one knee and kissed my hands.
>
>'Vous etes gentil, mon cher,' I said as I smiled down on my former lover and friend. 'Agar had to rush to the side of a wounded love and sent me to assume her part,' I said. "But Madame!" they sputtered. 'There is no other choice. I have far more to lose than you!'
>
>In that instant, the drum roll signaled Rouget de Lisle's impassioned anthem, and the entire audience had risen to its feet as I walked out onstage. Gasps of disbelief assailed me. Here was the Paris that had adored me, revered me, implored me, and now chosen to ignore me. I had all of their eyes and all of their ears as I stood before them, the most famous and most infamous woman of their world, as the first strains of the orchestra began "La Marseillaise" and my voice rang out those magical words:
>
>>Jans, enjants de Ja patrie. . .
>>le jour de gloire est arnve'.
>>Contre nous de la Tyrannie
>>l'e'tendard sanglant est leve'.

THE DIVINE RISING STAR - *by Robert W. Cabell*

SARAH
My life, my career, my love for my country, and my need for these people, galvanized into the power of my voice. It soared above the orchestra. And they soared with me and my passion for the words of freedom.

> Aux armes, citoyens!
> Formez vos bataillons!

The entire audience rose as one, like a wave cresting towards me, and joined their voices to mine.

> Liberte', Liberte' che'rie

As the orchestra swelled to a climactic crescendo, I flung my arms wide, and my gown, until then a shimmering swirl of red, white, and blue rivulets transformed into the French flag.
She flings her arms wide and the cloak she is wearing is lined with the French flag.

> Ton triomphe et notre gloire.

A thunderous roar enveloped me as I was assailed with accolades of my reclamation—reborn like a phoenix rising from the ashes of their ambivalence as their chosen one!

I am done, spent, and you have now heard how sad little Sarah, who fantasized as a babe in Brittany that her mother would someday come to love her, earned the love and devotion of France, England, and America.

SCENE VII - RECONCILIATION

SARAH
I had become the world's most famous star. I had become truly loved. And for the next forty-three years I would dedicate my life to nourish and continue that love. For, quand même, in spite of everything, love is the true measure of life!

END OF SHOW

SARAH IN HER DIVINE YOUNG ROLES

Sarah in her debut as *Iphigenia*

SARAH IN HER DIVINE YOUNG ROLES

Sarah as *Cleopatra* in "Cleopatra"

SARAH IN HER DIVINE YOUNG ROLES

Sarah as *Zanetto* in "Le Passant"

SARAH IN HER DIVINE YOUNG ROLES

Sarah as *The Little Queen* in "Ruy Blas"

SARAH IN HER DIVINE YOUNG ROLES

Sarah as *Donna Sol* in "Hermani"

SARAH IN HER DIVINE YOUNG ROLES

Sarah as *Phaedra* in "Phaedra"

SARAH IN HER DIVINE YOUNG ROLES

Sarah sleeping in her coffin

SARAH IN HER DIVINE YOUNG ROLES

Sarah Bernhardt as Fashion Icon of the 1800's

SARAH IN HER DIVINE YOUNG ROLES

Sarah as *Adrienne* in "Adrienne La Lecouvreur"

SARAH IN HER DIVINE YOUNG ROLES

Sarah as *Marguerite* in "La Dame aux Camelias"

SARAH IN HER DIVINE YOUNG ROLES

Sarah as *Gilbert* in "Frou-frou"

WILDE AND DIVINE

PART I OF THE DIVINE TRILOGY OF SARAH BERNHARDT

A CELEBRATION OF THE TWENTY YEAR FRIENDSHIP OF OSCAR WILDE AND SARAH BERNHARDT

A Play Robert W. Cabell

A Play by Robert W. Cabell

Directed by Robert W. Cabell

As Performed by
Terria Joseph and Peter McLean

WILDE AND DIVINE

As Produced in Reparatory at:

The Trilogy Theater
341 West 44thStreet
New York, NY 10036
In 2001

No part of this script may be used or reproduced by any means, graphic, electronic, or mechanical: including photocopying, recording, taping, or by any information storage retrieval system, without the written permission of the publisher, except in the case of brief quotations embodied in critical articles and reviews.

WILDE AND DIVINE
is dedicated to my friend,
Mikal Anderson, with whom I have had
a divine friendship for over forty years.

CHARACTERS

OSCAR WILDE:
Everything about Oscar *Fingal O'Flahertie Wills* Wilde was bigger than life. At an astonishing height of 6 feet 3 inches, in an era known for short men, he favored green overcoats, turquoise colored canes with white ivory tops, and a burgeoning boutonnière stuffed with large Casa Blanca Lilies or sunflowers. He was born the second son to Lord and Lady Wilde, and his father was the personal physician to Queen Victoria. While still a student at university, Oscar was fluent in French and German, and dubbed his idol, Sarah Bernhardt, with the title of "Divine." By the time he was thirty, Oscar had become world famous for his celebrated wit and his poetry, and toured as a lecturer in America on the philosophy of aestheticism, all before he wrote his first play or novel.

In 1890, at the age of thirty-six, he published "The Picture of Dorian Gray." In the early 1890's, Oscar wrote and produced such plays as , "The Importance of Being Ernest", "Lady Windermere's Fan", and "The Perfect Husband," and a collection of fairy tales that made him one of the most successful authors and playwrights of the Victorian era.

Though Oscar was happily married to his wife, Constance, and the father of two sons, he became involved in a decadent and romantic relationship with Lord Alfred Douglass, the young son of the Marques of Queensberry. For this, he was brought up and convicted on the charge of "Gross Indecency" and imprisoned for two years of hard
labor. During his incarceration, he wrote "De Profundis,"

a dichotomy of his early works of humor and wit, which elaborated on the dark sojourn of his trial and imprisonment. It was not published until five years after his death.

After his sentence was served, Oscar left England forever and moved to France. His health and pride never recovered from his brutal experience in prison, which he detailed in his piece, "The Ballad of Reading Gaol," in 1898, his last work. He saw the new century arrive, but died penniless in Paris at the age of forty-six, on November 3, 1900.

SARAH BERNHARDT:

Sarah Bernhardt's mother, aunt, and two sisters were celebrated courtesans of Paris and known for their great beauty. Sarah herself was considered thin and plain, but with an exceptionally rich and melodious speaking voice. Her reddish-blonde hair was thick, frizzy, and unruly, her arms overly long, her bust too small, and her nose too big. Yet when she walked onstage in the character of one of her fallen women, she imbued herself with a radiance and internal war of emotions that transformed her into the pinnacle of style and sensuality. She was the first woman to successfully portray the male role of Hamlet, and the only actress to receive rave reviews for both the roles of Hamlet and Ophelia.

Bernhardt embraced a personal life that was equally daring and dramatic. She slept in a coffin, traveled with a menagerie of wild and exotic animals, including panthers, rhinos and pythons, was the first woman to ride in a hot air balloon, hunted bears and crocodiles, and had a love of all things strange and macabre. Her onstage love scenes were equally matched by her torrid affairs, well into her 70's. Most of her leading men were her lovers, and her closest personal friend was a notorious lesbian. That combined with her sold out, salacious performances, made her the most famous woman in the world for over half a century.

Sarah was anti-drugs, anti-smoking, and vehemently against the death penalty in an era when civilization accepted all of those. Her circle of intimate friends included the greatest writers of her time, like Oscar Wilde, Alexander Dumas, Victor Hugo, Mark Twain, and royalty such as, Edward the Prince of Wales and his wife Princess Alexandra. The Czar of Russia knelt to her, a Belgium prince fathered her only child, and the Grand Duke of Austria vacated his castle for her use. President Teddy Roosevelt was a devoted fan, as well as some of the greatest intellectuals of her time such as, Edison, Tesla, and Freud.

At fifty she was convincingly portraying nineteen year old virgins, and her romantic scenes were both the rage and scandal of the civilized world. Dying on stage slowly, tortuously, languidly, and tragically, was her greatest specialty. Those who came after her desperately tried to mimic her poses and gestures which were organic to her unique talents. Those who mimicked her were judged as overly dramatic or cliché. No audience that saw Bernhardt "die," escaped the onslaught of the deep and overwhelming emotions she conveyed.

THE SET

"Wilde And Divine" takes place during a charity performance of Sarah Bernhardt's greatest scenes, hosted by Oscar Wilde. There are very few traditional "scenes" within the play so it is divided by "transitions" more than scenes, and they are interacting with the audience within the reality of the play, so it is in fact a play within a play, with scenes from many plays.

The set is very minimal. Across the length of far backstage, is a two foot high, four foot wide platform that runs the width of the stage. There's a four foot wide, three step set of stairs in the center, that allows ample room for entrance and exit space for one or more persons, and an adaptable playing area.

The stage should be framed with a classical, draped proscenium arch. Upstage left, down stage of the platform, there is a large tri-fold dressing screen, decorated by images of Mucha theatrical posters of Sarah. To balance the set, far stage right and down stage of the platforms, there is a pedestal or a high oval table with two glasses and two decanters and a scattering of silver framed photos. A large, decorative, wooden armchair left of center and a long, wide, sturdy, backless bench center stage right, are the only other furniture necessary. Lights and costumes create the variety for the production. Full costumes changes for each character are orchestrated of stage during solo narratives of either Sarah or Oscar. Sarah will add or subtract costume accessories, like shawls, hats, gloves and fans using the dressing screen.

WILDE and DIVINE
Part II of The Divine Trilogy
Of Sarah Bernhardt
by
Robert W. Cabell

SCENE I

ODE TO SARAH

(OSCAR enters carrying a glass of champagne.)

OSCAR
For those of you who haven't read your programs or have already had too much to drink - I am Oscar Wilde. *(Crosses down the center stair to downstage center.)* The reason we are assembled here tonight is to pay tribute to the Divine Sarah Bernhardt! Now, since it's beyond rude that you all started drinking without me, let me propose a toast! *(OSCAR raises his glass of champagne aloft.)* Mark Twain said, "There are five kinds of actresses: bad actresses, fair actresses, good actresses, great actresses - and then there is Sarah Bernhardt." George Bernard Shaw, a self-made man who adored his maker wrote: "She lives to mesmerize, to dazzle, to lure the public into the mysteries of sensuality and poetic illusion."
(Crosses to stage right to bench.)
D.H. Lawrence claimed– "She is fascinating to an extraordinary

WILDE AND DIVINE – By Robert W. Cabell

OSCAR
degree." "She is the incarnation of wild emotion". *(OSCAR winks and chuckles as he surveys the audience and then continues as if he is sharing a wicked secret.)*
Sigmund Freud's infatuation with Sarah was more than evident to all who entered his office. There he prominently displayed a portrait of Bernhardt -- with his own quote: "Every inch of that little figure lives and bewitches. Every limb and joint acts with her." Anyone who ever said, "A Penny for your thoughts" – was never psychoanalyzed by Freud. *(Crosses right to gesture to the dressing screen.)* In 1872 after her first performance as the little queen in "Ruy Blas", the great Victor Hugo knelt at her feet. In 1874 on her opening night as Doña Sol in *Hernani*, Hugo claimed the tear of gratitude he wept – crystallized in to a diamond, which he presented to her the next evening on a gold bracelet. The Czar of all Russia knelt to her, the Prince of Wales befriended her, and a prince of Belgium sired her only son. In short, all the great men of her era, be they princes, czars, poets, or generals, - "all" - became eager lovers and little boys when blessed with her presence.
(OSCAR laughs softly then crosses downstage center.)
Things of mystery and light tend to turn to brass or become mundane when held up to scrutiny. Few could equal or surpass the expectations of a maddening crowd. A siren, a goddess, a rose by any other name that we call Sarah– an immortal beauty

SCENE I – ODE TO SARAH

OSCAR *(cont'd)*
>that defied explanation, to cast a legendary shadow of elegance and sensuality across light years, to become "Divine." *(OSCAR raises his glass of champagne in a circular motion around the room.)* To the Divine Sarah!

(OSCAR then drains his glass, crosses to the pedestal upstage right, places the empty glass on it, and then crosses down to the bench and sits facing the audience.)

>The first time I ever saw Sarah – I was a student at Oxford in Paris on Holliday. Her name was on the lips of all the young intellectuals and artist. *(OSCAR rises opening his arms with an expansive gesture and twirls around with an excited air.)* And so I found myself high in the back of a balcony, my giant frame crushed *(clutches arms inward)* against the wiry French frames of my friends gazing down on this elfin beauty. It was her performance of Victor Hugo's sad Little Queen in *Ruy Blas,* and she crept inside the heart of the audience filling it with a sad and tender ache for love unfulfilled.

(OSCAR backs up to the platform upstage right and sits.)

(SARAH enters extreme upstage left on the platform, dressed as the LITTLE QUEEN in ivory velvet with a trailing white lace shawl and a white lace collar. She hurries nervously across the platform, down the stairs to far downstage right then turns and calls quickly over her shoulder.)

WILDE AND DIVINE – By Robert W. Cabell

SARAH (*as the Little Queen*)

LITTLE QUEEN

Casilda! I know what I say. That man – *(she points back offstage right)* is my bad angel. *(Shudders and crosses herself.)*. On the morning of his downfall I sat as usual to receive the grandees. Don Salluste came with the rest. Slowly he glided towards me, fingering his dagger, which he half drew. I saw the blade gleam but the light in his eyes was more deadly still, and his kiss on my hand *(holds her hand away from her in repulsion)* like the icy touch of embodied venom. *(SARAH whirls away and takes a step upstage left and then turns back to face the downstage corner where Casilda is placed.)* I wish I could. *(She rubs at the top of her wrist as if to clean away a stain.)* That kiss – poison. *(Looks up and out as if recalling the whole scene.)* And Don Salluste's smoldering eyes, at times, too, when he is least in my mind, *(moves nervously)* menace me from curtained nooks and shadowy corners. *(SARAH looks down stage right in a plea of help.)* Whilst he lives there will be no end of his hatred for me, Casilda.

SCENE I – ODE TO SARAH

(Lights goes blue and then fade out on SARAH as they cross fade to OSCAR sitting on the bench and she exits in the dark.)

OSCAR
When the night was over – I was swept along with a group of students that unhitched the horses from her personal carriage –- and that night the Divine one was drawn through the gas lit streets of Paris by a herd of cheering, adoring fans, drunk from her splendor, singing her praises at the top of our slightly inebriated lungs.

(OSCAR races up the center stairs to the platform and ends by waving off as if Sarah is leaving.)

Thus in September of 1880, when Sarah first arrived upon the far shores of England beneath the white cliffs of Dover *(OSCAR walks down the stairs to stand at the base of the stairs stage right of center)*, I was there with another mob of adoring fans – waving and chanting her personal motto, "Quand meme", which had become a veritable by-word for young artistic-intellectuals. *(OSCAR strolls across the left of center, smugly.)* For the cretins among you that don't speak French, "Quand meme" stands for "in spite of everything" as in "I will succeed" or "As God is my witness I shall never go hungry again!" *(Smiles and take a beat.)* So - there we were, *(OSCAR crosses back just right of center)* crowding the dock to greet our Sarah, as the rest of the Comédie-Française de-boarded their ship. I stepped forward with an armful

OSCAR *(cont'd)*
of lilies, welcoming her on behalf of several Oxford alumni—

(As SARAH enters far upstage left, OSCAR takes a step forward and is carrying an armful of flowers.)

and I cast a bouquet at her feet, which elicited tumultuous cheers from the crowd.

(SARAH acknowledges OSCAR with a smile as he mimes casting the lilies upon the ground in front of her feet as he smiles back at the audience.)

SARAH
Your charming welcome, Oscar dear, also imported a ship load of disgruntled frowns from my fellow company members.

OSCAR
You see the Comédie had no star system and Sarah had just recently returned to the fold after a ten years absence.

SARAH
I originally joined the company at seventeen, straight from the conservatory—

OSCAR
—and left a year later and after slapping an established actress—

SCENE I – ODE TO SARAH

SARAH
>—for shoving my little sister Regina into a column, and bloodying her poor little nose. I was told to either apologize or leave. I left!

OSCAR
>—only to return ten years later from the Odeon Theatre when she had become the darling of Paris.

SARAH
>The fact that I was getting so much attention—

OSCAR
>—loosed the green-eyed monster named jealousy amongst the Comédie.

SARAH
(Laughs.)

OSCAR
>The monster grew fangs and doubled in size when the scheduled opening night was submitted—

SARAH
>—and it did not include a performance of mine.

(SARAH and OSCAR. counter cross leaving OSCAR downstage right of center and SARAH downstage left of center.)

WILDE AND DIVINE – By Robert W. Cabell

OSCAR
> It sprouted wings and breathed fire when London announced that if Madame Sarah did not perform on the opening night – the entire contract would be canceled.

SARAH
> There was no such thing as petty jealousy at the Comédie-Française, - they did everything in a grand manner.

(OSCAR steps just right of center above the thrust semi circle.)

OSCAR
> However, the Comédie Manager ,M. Perrine, abhorred the idea of canceling a very lucrative engagement, so—

SARAH
(SARAH steps to just left of center mirroring OSCAR)
> —the gala opening was rescheduled to include my performance of the second act of Jean Racine's *Phaedra*—

OSCAR
> —the second wife of Theseus, king of Athens.

SCENE I – ODE TO SARAH

SARAH
>It is the story of a young Greek queen consumed with passion for her stepson and wracked with guilt that annihilates her virtue and sunders her soul.

(SARAH sweeps around stage left circling back up far upstage center preparing herself as she raises her shawl up over her head and trails it across her arms.)

OSCAR
>For which I – *(OSCAR gestures off to SARAH as he slowly backs off to the upstage right corner next to the screen)* – was in the audience that night.

(OSCAR steps behind the screen and disappears as the lights cross fade from him to SARAH upstage center.)

SARAH *(as PHEADRA)*

PHEADRA

>My husband lives!
>Oenone; - I understand!
>I have confessed a love he will abhor.
>He lives, and have I wronged him.
>Say no more!
>I foresaw this, but you changed my course.
>Your tears won out over my just remorse.
>I might have died this morning,
>mourned and chaste.
>I took your counsels and I die disgraced.
>Just Heaven! Think what I have done!
>My husband's coming;

WILDE AND DIVINE – By Robert W. Cabell

PHEADRA *(cont'd)*

with him will be his son.
I'll see the witness of my vile desire.
Watch with what countenance
I can greet his sire,
my heart still heavy
with rejected sighs, and tears
which could not move him in my eyes.
Mindful of Theseus' honor,
will Hypolitus conceal
the scandal of my passion, do you feel?
Deceiving both his sire and king?
Will he contain the horror
that he feels for me?
His silence would be vain!

What ill I've done I know, Oenone,
and I am not one of those bold women who,
at ease in crime are never seen
to blush at any time.
I know my mad deeds, I recall them all.
I think that in this place each vault,
each wall can speak, and that,
impatient to accuse,
they wait to give my trusting spouse
their news.
I'll die, then;
from these horrors I'll be free.
Is it so sad a thing to cease to be?
Death is not fearful to a suffering mind.

SCENE I – ODE TO SARAH

PHEADRA *(cont'd)*

My only fear's the name I leave behind
for my poor children,
what a dire bequest!
Each has the blood of Jove within his breast.
But whatsoever pride of blood they share,
A mother's crime's a heavy thing to bear.
I tremble lest – alas, too truly!
– they be chided
for their mother's guilt some day.
I tremble lest, befouled by such a stain
neither should dare to lift his head again

(The lights fade out on SARAH as she sits rocking herself slowly like a wounded child.)

SCENE II

BY THE LIGHT OF THE SILVERY MOON

(The lights rise on OSCAR standing in front of a screen far upstage.)

OSCAR
> That night Sarah became the darling of London and she would maintain that bond of love for another forty years. Anything she performed in immediately sold out, eclipsing everyone else within the Comédie – with whom she would soon part company.

(The lights rise back on SARAH as she moves downstage left of center and OSCAR mirrors her move.)

SARAH
> But it was long before London that the pot began to boil.

OSCAR
> The Comédie-Française had two goddesses to grace its stage. The lusciously curvaceous and easygoing Sophie Croizette, and the exotic, willowy, and willful Sarah Bernhardt.

SARAH
> Perrine had wanted me to join the Comédie for my box office name, but he was smitten if not dottily devoted to Sophie Croizette. He gave her all the lum lead roles and usually relegated me to obscurity—

SCENE II – BY THE LIGHT OF THE SILVERY MOON

OSCAR

—something her fans and the critics were all unhappy with.

SARAH

Finally, he decided to give me a role to create in Octave Feuillet's play, *Le Sphinx*.

OSCAR

Once again, Sophie was cast in the principal role of Blanche.

SARAH

But, in fact, *(she crosses far left stage standing next to the bench)* the role I was cast in was more to my liking. *(Sarah sits up on it.)* I was Bertha, the wounded, almost heroic wife and betrayed friend. I decided it had all the necessary substance to become the real principle role, and this soon became evident during our early rehearsals.

OSCAR

The scenes seemed to suddenly revolve around Sarah's character. Even when she was not there, the character left its presence on stage like the lingering fragrance of a rare perfume.

SARAH

Perrine began to get nervous, and Sophie was not as attentive when she sulked in her dressing room.

WILDE AND DIVINE – By Robert W. Cabell

OSCAR
(Crosses far downstage center.)
In act three, across a footbridge in a moonlight garden, Sophie's character, in what was in those times a daring kiss *(he crosses back upstage left of the screen)*…attempted to destroy the marriage of her best friend by seducing her husband.

SARAH
A few moments later my character entered. But I advanced slowly and forlorn, with my pale shoulders and bare arms glistening in the moonlight… *(circles down around the stage)* …trailing my wrap like a pale forgotten shroud behind me, and created quite a vision. Sophie gasped at the effect, and Perrine suddenly shouted.

OSCAR *(as PERRINE)*
Kill the moon effect, it is for Sophie alone and should not be used for Sarah.

SARAH *(in the past)*
'Oh no, Monsieur Perrine, you will not take away my moon. The manuscript reads, "Berthe enters, convulse with emotion, pale beneath the rays of the moon." I am pale and I am convulsed with emotion – and I will have my moon or I will not perform.' *(SARAH exits.)*

SCENE II – BY THE LIGHT OF THE SILVERY MOON

OSCAR
Of course Perrine tried to replace Sarah with other actresses—
(SARAH reenters.)

SARAH
One of them was an actress we called "the crocodile." She followed all the principals around memorizing their lines, hoping to jump in and seize their part at the first sign of illness or trouble.

OSCAR
But the playwright would not accept them, and after two days of absence, Sarah returned with her moon. Sarah not only triumphed in the part of Berthe—

SARAH
I took over the role of Blanche and toured the world with it, making a much greater success of it than Sophie ever did.

OSCAR
But from that day in March 1874 forward, Perrine bore an open grudge against Sarah.

SARAH
I was summoned to the Comédie to hear *Rome Vaincue*, and to Perrine's surprise and bridled delight, I refused the principal role of Ompimia, the young vestal virgin.

WILDE AND DIVINE – By Robert W. Cabell

OSCAR *(as PERRINE)*
   What does our vexing little Bernhardt want now? The principal role is no longer enough?

SARAH *(in the past)*
   'I wish to play the role of Fosthumia.'

OSCAR *(as PERRINE)*
   'A seventy-year-old hag? Are you mad!'

SARAH *(in the past)*
   'For once, I am not asking for the principal role. You should be happy!'

OSCAR *(as PERRINE)*
   'Anything to not have to hear you complain to the ministry behind my back. But who would play opposite you? It would have to be an actor of equal note.'

SARAH *(in the past)*
   'Mounet Sully can play old Vestapor, and your precious equilibrium will be restored.'

OSCAR *(as PERRINE)*
   'If you wish to make a fool of yourself, please mademoiselle – be my guest!..'

(SARAH slowly crosses to the bench.)

SCENE II – BY THE LIGHT OF THE SILVERY MOON

SARAH
But I did not make a fool of myself. I had taken up sculpting and painting to fill my hours of frustration, and many of those were spent with an old woman whom I had met on the cliffs of the ocean. She was casting bread onto the crashing

SARAH *(cont'd)*
waves below. She had lost her sons to the sea, and recently her young grandson. With each shredded crumb, she sent prayers and offerings to their souls with this peasant symbolism. I befriended her, I sculpted her, I knew her pain. I had etched the lines of sorrow and carved those eyes that saw far away and beyond. She was my Fosthumia. It was an ordinary piece of theater in which Sully and I were an extraordinary success.

OSCAR
(Upstage left of stage.)
This success led to Sarah and Mounet being cast opposite each other in *Hernani*.

SARAH
Once again it was a Victor Hugo play that would raise me to glory, in the role of Doña Sol.

(SARAH crosses far downstage center and takes character of DOÑA SOL. She holds a shielded candle aloft and looks offstage right as if peering into the night searching for someone.)

DOÑA SOL
Is that you, Hernani?

(OSCAR, stage left, dons a wide black brim hat and dark cloak, and comes up behind her as DON CARLOS.)

DON CARLOS
A voice more loving you could never wish.
It is a lover's voice; the lover is the king.
(DOÑA SOL flinches at his touch and whirls stage right.)

DOÑA SOL
The king!

DON CARLOS
(Kneeling.) Oh! Speak, command! A kingdom's thine! For he whose tender fetters thou shouldst break your lord, the king; *(takes her hand and pulls in for an attempted kiss)* tis Carlos now thy slave.

(She tries to pull free from his grasp.)

DOÑA SOL
(Yanks her hand back.)
Hernani, help!
(He pulls her back to him and holds her fiercely.)

DON CARLOS
Thou art affrighted! 'Tis not thy bandit holds thee, but the king.

SCENE II – BY THE LIGHT OF THE SILVERY MOON

(She yanks free then holds herself up regally and turns her body away from him as far as she can.)

DOÑA SOL
You are the bandit! Fie on you, for shame, you make the blush rise hotly to my cheeks!

(He laughs at her, then she continues speaking.)

Is such an action worthy of a king? To steal by force a woman in the night! Hernani's worth a hundred such as you. I call him king whose soul proclaims him such, and if the heart alone made king and bandit too, to him would fall the scepter and to you the dirk.

(DON CARLOS goes to her and grabs her.)

DON CARLOS
Madame! *(He tries to draw her to him again, as she keeps struggling.)*

DOÑA SOL
Do you forget my father was a count?

DON CARLOS
I'll make you a duchess.

WILDE AND DIVINE – By Robert W. Cabell

DOÑA SOL
Go away for shame! No bond could ever be 'twixt you and me. My aged father gave his life-blood for you. Of noble blood am I, and stand too high to be your mistress, too low to be your queen.

DON CARLOS
No, come share my throne and bear my name! I'll make you queen – nay, empress.

DOÑA SOL
It is a snare! I've pledged, as woman will, my life and soul, in bond irrevocable by human power, though tongue had never shaped it, and rather would I share Hernani's fortune, even at its bleakest – cold, abandonment, war, exile, beggary, and worst of all, the scourge, great king, of thine immaculate justice, than be enthroned an empress with an emperor.

(OSCAR removes his cape as he speaks)

OSCAR
It was easy to see how a man could sacrifice anything for the love of her Doña Sol.

(OSCAR folds his cape around the hat as he slips them both into the trunk.)

SCENE II – BY THE LIGHT OF THE SILVERY MOON

OSCAR
Sarah's success in that role was so great, that for many years to come, Doña Sol would become a synonym for Sarah Bernhardt.

SARAH slowly exits behind the screen.)

So much so, that in 1885, when Victor Hugo died, Sarah donned a black dress and veil to anonymously follow the hearse on foot with the rest of Paris.

OSCAR
One by one the crowd recognized her and respectfully took a few steps back. So, in the end it was Sarah – alone – walking mournfully behind the horse drawn coffin of her artistic master with all of Paris following Hugo and his lovely Doña Sol.

༺༻༺༻༺༻༺༻༺༻༺༻

SCENE III

ON DISTANT SHORES

OSCAR
Sarah's life was a stream of extraordinary moments, full of extraordinary people attracted to her exotic style and irrepressible humor. The fact that Sarah ever accepted an invitation to tour America totally amazed me.

(SARAH enters.)

SARAH
Many of my admirers and most of the papers of Europe claimed it was merely for the sake of acquiring obscene amounts of money–

OSCAR
– which no one could make like Sarah.

SARAH
Oscar! You also toured America, two years after me!

OSCAR
– but only out of financial deference. If one had the money to go to America, one would not go.

SARAH
But it is a lovely country and they swarmed to the theater.

SCENE III – ON DISTANT SHORES

OSCAR
> They're like mindless insects – they'd swarm to anything! But to Americans, art has no marvel, beauty, no meaning, and the past, no message.

SARAH
> Sailing off to America didn't fill you with a sense of adventure?

OSCAR
> The trip was slow, dull, and uneventful. I was disappointed with the Atlantic Ocean. Having heard of your treatment by customs, when they asked me if I had anything to declare I replied, 'I have nothing to declare but my genius.'

SARAH
> My company and I also toured several French cities in Canada–

OSCAR
> –something which I never bothered with.

SARAH
> We caused quite a stir in Montreal.

OSCAR
> Very Catholic up there you know, into virtue and penitence. Something you'd never catch me at – though I love the robes, the purses, and the incense.

WILDE AND DIVINE – By Robert W. Cabell

SARAH
 In Montreal, the Bishop was completely incensed with the roles of fallen women I portrayed, and threatened, preached, and damned me so severely…

OSCAR
 – that the entire country rushed to see you. They made up a charming poem about it.

> A Bishop – this is no canard –
> His parishioners put on their guard:
> Said he, "If you go to Sara B's show,
> In the world that's to come you'll burn hard."
>
> His flock at the prospect was sad
> For a moment, but then it got mad,
> And when Sarah did act,
> The hall was so packed,
> That standing room couldn't be had.

OSCAR
 And Sarah remarked,

SARAH
> 'Bless his eyes.
> In my bosom no malice there lies.
> The Bishop knew not,
> When he launched that curse hot
> That me, he would just advertise.'

SCENE III – ON DISTANT SHORES

OSCAR
A bit rough around the edges, but it has a catchy phrase or two. So – I avoided all that and enjoyed New York, which, like Sarah said, is a Masculine city. And there, – trying to measure my manners against my masculinity, several young men of society took me on a tour of brothels to view proof of my male prowess–

SARAH
– for which in both bed and booze – I heard – you gave ample proof.

OSCAR
I was torn to bits by society there.

SARAH
All those immense receptions, wonderful dinners, crowds – waiting for your carriage.

OSCAR
I waved a gloved hand and an ivory cane and they cheered. I generally behaved as I have always behaved–

SARAH
– dreadfully.

OSCAR
I could never see what you saw in it. One thing in America that sent Sarah into absolute rapture was Niagara Falls.

WILDE AND DIVINE – By Robert W. Cabell

SARAH
>   For many years I had dreamed of seeing Niagara Falls, and my tour of America finally brought that dream to pass. The deafening sound of the cataracts seemed like music, and the limpidity of the silvery cascades were pictures in my mind I was soon to see with my own eyes. What shall I say of the falls? I remained more than an hour. My eyes filled with tears as I stood there on the balcony hollowed out of the rock, memorized by the splendor of the sight. A radiant sun made the air around us iridescent. There were rainbows everywhere, lighting up the atmosphere with their soft colors. The pendants of hard ice hanging along the rocks on each side looked like enormous jewels. I gazed upon the scene, bewildered and fascinated by the rapid movement of the water, which looked like a wide, unfolding sheet of silver, dashed constantly into a rebounding, splashing heap, with a noise unlike any sound we had ever heard. What marvelous grandeur!

OSCAR
>   As a devotee of the Divine One, I hate to disagree. But to me, Niagara Falls is a vast unnecessary amount of water going the wrong way and then falling over unnecessary rocks.

SCENE III – ON DISTANT SHORES

SARAH
It's a very romantic place, Oscar. It's been a favorite place for American honeymoons for years.

OSCAR
Then it must be one of the earliest, if not the keenest disappointments of American married life. I never shared your love of flora and fauna, my dear. I never understood how you could be the personification of beauty and grace on stage, and a veritable Diana of the Hunt off.

SARAH
I love horseback riding, hot air ballooning, crocodile hunting in the bayous, or shooting birds for breakfast. I adore badminton and croquette before lunch and puttering around my garden in the late afternoon.

OSCAR
All with such annoying zealous glee! I take my fruit in the form of preserves and my favorite vegetable is carrot cake. Man is at his best when he is civilized – and so is a vegetable. Speaking of civilization – like the rest of England, I simply laugh at Americans and think it divine retribution for me to tour the states and be paid vast amounts of money for the fruitless tasks of lecturing to them on aesthetics and manners. But Sarah's American tour bore the fruit of genius.

WILDE AND DIVINE – By Robert W. Cabell

SARAH
One of the eight plays I had prepared for my reparatory was an old play that I myself had never before performed in and was a last minute choice. I was still looking for the last play.

(SARAH crosses down to OSCAR who is readying to become PIERRE BERTON)

OSCAR *(as PIERRE)*
Now Sarah, I want you to read *La Dame aux Camélias*, by Alexander Dumas. *(He hands her a book.)*

SARAH *(in the past)*
The play is twenty-eight years old, Pierre. It has never had any great success in any theater or for any actress who starred in it.

OSCAR *(as PIERRE)*
Sarah, you have the illusive sensuality to make this role a classic! You can make this part live like it has never lived before. Trust me. Read it.

SARAH *(in the past)*
(Crosses down far stage left.) But Pierre, isn't it the part of a courtesan? It is much too close to home. I have enough troubles with the papers as it is without dragging my family business – literally – on to the stage with me.

SCENE III – ON DISTANT SHORES

OSCAR *(as PIERRE)*
(Stands.) But you will triumph in it! *(Crosses.)*

SARAH *(in the past)*
'I'll read it, Pierre, but I will make no promises.'
(OSCAR crosses to the bench behind her and places the book down.)

OSCAR *(as PIERRE)*
Just read it, and you will see that I am right.
(OSCAR moves upstage right of the screen.)

SARAH
(SARAH Crosses down left.)
And he was. It was like reading the diary of my dear, sweet sister Regina. She had lived the life of a courtesan – as had my mother and my aunt – and had died of consumption and her morphine addiction at the age of eighteen. So lovely. So tragic. *(Crosses far down left.)* The last few months of her life, I slept beside her and took care of her every need. Oh, I knew what others could never know, and – in a very real way – Marguerite *was* Regina. Here was my chance to create a character of great depth and longing, full of noble sacrifice.

OSCAR
(OSCAR enters and places a chair upstage center.)
On November 16, 1880, at New York's Booth Theater, Sarah debuted a role that she would portray in over 3,000 performances in her lifetime – and

WILDE AND DIVINE – By Robert W. Cabell

OSCAR *(cont'd)*
created one of the most extraordinary and enduring depictions in theatrical history –Marguerite, from *La Dame aux Camélias*.

(OSCAR takes on the character of ARMAND and SARAH takes on the character of MARGUERITE.)

MARGUERITE
Armand! *(She throws herself into his arms and clings to him.)* It cannot be you. It is impossible that God should be so good to me!

ARMAND
(Kneeling.) It is I, Marguerite – so repentant. My father wrote me everything! I did not know where to go to hide from my love and my remorse. I went off like a mad man, traveling day and night without respite, without sleep, pursued by terrible forebodings, seeing from afar your house draped in black!

MARGUERITE
You are not returning to your same pretty little Marguerite, but I am still young. I will grow lovely again, now that I am happy. You will forget everything. From today on, we will begin life all over again!

SCENE III – ON DISTANT SHORES

ARMAND
I am never leaving you again. Listen, Marguerite, we are going to leave this house at once – we will never see Paris again.

ARMAND *(cont'd)*
My father knows what you are – he will love you as the good angel of his son. My sister is married – the future is ours.

MARGUERITE
Oh – speak to me! Speak to me! I feel my soul being reborn with your every word! You are breathing new health into me. I was saying this morning, one and only one thing could save me. I did not dare hope for it – and here you are!

ARMAND
I love you, Marguerite. All my life belongs to you. *(She reels, and only ARMAND'S hand holding her tightly keeps her from falling.)* Marguerite – what is it? You are so white...

MARGUERITE
Nothing, dear, nothing. It is just that joy does not so suddenly come into a despairing heart without straining it a little. *(She sits down and throws her head back.)*

WILDE AND DIVINE – By Robert W. Cabell

ARMAND
Marguerite – speak to me!

MARGUERITE
(Coming back to herself.) Do not be afraid, dearest; you know that I have always been subject to these silly spells of fainting. But they pass quickly. Look at me – I am smiling – I am strong! It is the surprise of being alive that weighs on me!

ARMAND
(He takes her hand.) You are trembling.

MARGUERITE
It is nothing! Nanine – come, Nanine. Hurry – give me a cape, a hat.

ARMAND
(With terror.) My God – my God!

MARGUERITE
(She tries to walk and stumbles back.)
I cannot. *(Throws off her cape angrily.)*

ARMAND
Nanine! Run! Fetch the doctor!

SCENE III – ON DISTANT SHORES

MARGUERITE
Yes, yes. Tell him Armand has come back, that I want to live! *(She smiles weakly as her eyes follow Nanine.)* But if your return has not saved me, nothing will save me.

MARGUERITE
Sooner or later, man must die of that which made him live. I lived on love – I am dying of it.

ARMAND
Do not say such things, Marguerite; you will live – you must!

MARGUERITE
Sit by me, close, my love, and listen to me carefully. *(He sits by her as she gently brushes back a lock of his hair from his forehead.)* A moment ago I rebelled angrily against death! I am sorry…Death is necessary, and I am grateful to it, since it waited until you came to strike me. Had my death not been certain, your father would not have written and asked you to return.

ARMAND
Listen, Marguerite, do not talk that way. Do you want to make me crazy!

WILDE AND DIVINE – By Robert W. Cabell

MARGUERITE
Even if I did not wish it, my dearest, I would be obliged to give in, since God wishes it. And if I had been a good girl, if everything within me were pure, then perhaps I might cry at the idea of leaving a world where you are to remain, because . the future would be filled with brightness and all my past would give me a right to them. But dead, all that you will keep of me will be pure; alive there would always be stains upon my love. Believe me, God does know what he is doing.

(OSCAR releases his character of ARMAND, smiles and squeezes SARAH's hand, then steps away from her and turns to the audience.)

OSCAR
And so did Sarah, when it came to illuminating the stage with a love scene or dying with a power and grace that wrenched tears from a blind man. She was a true artistic treasure – and for this very reason, the French were incredibly outraged lambasting her for casting the pearls of French literature before herds of swine consisting of Yankee millionaires, illiterate cowboys, and blanketed Indians.

SCENE IV

FOR THE LOVE OF MONEY

OSCAR
>You may be interested to hear that I have met Indians whose conversations were most intriguing so long as they were unintelligible. And out of reverence to the Irishman in me, I have also met coal miners. They are big-footed, red-shirted, yellow bearded, delightful ruffians. As for cowboys, I passed through St. Joseph Missouri two weeks after Jesse James was murdered and witnessed an auction where his possessions were being sold for a fortune.

(OSCAR crosses to the pedestal and pours himself a drink)
>I went to California. It's like Italy without the art. I lectured in Salt Lake City to the Mormons. It was the driest city I have ever been to and that doesn't count the weather or the salt.

(OSCAR drains his glass and sets it back down)
>The president was a nice old fellow with five wives. The penalty for bigamy in Utah – is multiple mother-in-laws.

(OSCAR Walks down center stage and peers into the audience)
>Are there any gentlemen in the audience tonight willing to pay that penalty? Hmmm – I thought not. *(Shrugs)* In my continued journey I went to Griggsville, Illinois – they asked me to lecture on aesthetics. I said they could begin by changing the name of their town. *(Crosses far down stage left)*

WILDE AND DIVINE – By Robert W. Cabell

OSCAR *(cont'd)*
I, like Sarah, had the misfortune to cross the Mississippi river during a flood. No well-behaved river ought to act that way. New Orleans was of course French, and quite civilized, with suitably decadent delights for ones palate. I also engaged in a few of those Negro Voodoo rites, something Sarah told me about and I had to see for myself. In New Orleans they call a soulless man a zombie. In England, we call him a critic.

(OSCAR slowly crosses far down stage left to center as he speaks)

America is like an unattractive woman – much more pleasing under the influence of alcohol. *(Oscar points to a woman in the audience)* Now there is a true American beauty. You know my dear, a woman should never complicate her beauty with intelligence, and I'm sure there is nothing complicated about you. *(Winks.)* They claim some clever American woman, once said, "If you can't say anything nice about someone, come sit by me." I'm sure that creature and I were soul mates in another life. Where else but in Texas could they have a real live murderess – playing Lady Macbeth. Her name on the program was followed by, "Ten years penal servitude." However back in London, Sarah Bernhardt was making waves with her "American Export" of *La Dame aux Camélias*.

SCENE V

LOVE'S LABORS LOST

(SARAH re-enters in a long, flowing, hooded robe tied with a belt around the waist, and full-length flowing sleeves, covering her SAINT JOAN costume and her hair, which is now a short jaw-length bob, for the next two monologues.)

OSCAR
    Ellen Terry, the great English actress, after watching this exquisite interpretation of Marguerite Gauthier said, "No one dies like Sarah B." In fact, Ellen and I got in the habit of stopping by and catching Sarah's death scenes from the wings or orchestra pit.

SARAH
    And Ellen, a good country girl, even if she was the toast of London, was usually carrying a basket of eggs or a bag of vegetables under her arm as she'd stop by on her way home from the market. After the show, she would sit and have tea and biscuits with me in my dressing room, along with Mrs. Patrick Campbell and John Henry Irving.

OSCAR
    By now Mademoiselle Bernhardt had built up a cult of London worshippers. The public collected her photographs, young girls kept scrapbooks of her press notices, and all the young actresses memorized her roles and imitated her every move and gesture.

SARAH
>I attracted all the lunatics of the world.

OSCAR
>We told her of a spinster who set up an altar in her rooms, consecrated solely to "The Divine One," displaying various objects Sarah had touched.

SARAH
>A pair of gloves, a handkerchief, a hair pin–

OSCAR
>– in addition to every known photograph ever taken of you. *(He laughs.)*

SARAH
>Don't make fun of her! I love her very much – though she probably drinks!

OSCAR
>The European tour which followed England led first through middle France and continued on as the Bernhardt legend blazed across Northern Italy–

SARAH
>– Greece–

OSCAR
>– Hungary–

SCENE V– LOVE'S LABORS LOST

SARAH
– Switzerland–

OSCAR
– Belgium–

SARAH
– and Holland. Masses mobbed my every hotel and train station stop–

OSCAR
– straining to catch a glimpse of The Divine One when they could not afford to attend a performance.

SARAH
In Scandinavia, I was so touched when a tiny hamlet petitioned to have my train slowed down so they could tell their grandchildren they had seen Sarah Bernhardt waving through the window. *(Giggles and then laughs.)*

OSCAR
It was the last era of royalty, and Sarah was the toast of the Austria of the Hapsburgs, the Spain of the Bourbons, and the Russia of the Romanovs. However, she refused any and all petitions to perform in Germany.

WILDE AND DIVINE – By Robert W. Cabell

SARAH
Oui! After the Siege of Paris, would I defile my hands with Prussian money? The very hands that Victor Hugo kissed?

OSCAR
In Russia, she was invited to perform at the Winter Palace.

SARAH
After my first performance, Czar Alexander III came backstage to greet me. I was shocked and very honored as I rushed forward to make a deep and reverent curtsy, and he stopped me.

OSCAR *(as ALEXANDER kneels)*
Non, Madame, it is I who must bow to you.

SARAH
(SARAH sits on his knee.) And he did, before his entire court. The incident caused a lot of talk among high society, especially after I was named France's official Ambassadress of Goodwill.
(Both rise.)

OSCAR
But His Imperial Majesty's gesture of homage to an actress was not the only topic of gossip concerning Mademoiselle Bernhardt. For if the Russian capital was the scene of one of her great professional victories–

SCENE V– LOVE'S LABORS LOST

SARAH
– it was also the setting for my private Waterloo.
(SARAH and OSCAR begin to move center, one line at a time.)

OSCAR
Her soon to be husband was a Greek tragedy in the form of a diplomat by the name of Aristides Damala.

SARAH
The scandal columns were filled with news of his paramours and wild escapades, and a titillated society summed him up as being a combination of Casanova–

OSCAR
– and the Marquis de Sade!

SARAH
The moment I set eyes on him–

OSCAR
(Puts his arm around her.) – Sarah's divinity deserted her, and she became all too mortal, both in life and her career.

SARAH
When Damala let fall the remark that if he had ever had one ambition in life, it might have been to act–
(She steps away.)

WILDE AND DIVINE – By Robert W. Cabell

OSCAR
– like the spellbound Titania, smitten with the ass-headed Bottom, Sarah suggested–

SARAH
– he read a scene with me from *Frou-frou*–

OSCAR
– which led to a little fal-da-rah, landed him in her bed for a lot of fiddle-de-dee, and climaxed with a job in her company. Yes, dear friends Monsieur Damala made the grand sacrifice of forsaking the political arena for the footlights.

SARAH
That is when he changed his first name to Jacques. He was my Beauty and my Beast.

OSCAR
Beastly was the best way to describe his acting both on and off the stage–

SARAH
– and I was as blind and addicted to him as he was to his morphine.

OSCAR
God knows what the man had between his legs, but it had to be a lot more than he had between his ears.

SCENE V– LOVE'S LABORS LOST

SARAH
It was a case of the blind leading – the blinded!

OSCAR
Unfortunately, before Sarah returned to her senses, she exacerbated her life by marrying the cretin in London in 1882.

SARAH
While I was rehearsing *Fédora*, my marriage reached a crisis.

OSCAR
Sardou, who was the grand maestro of the great successes of her grand career, resolutely refused to let Damala act in his play–

SARAH
– which sent Jacques into a rage and our marriage into turmoil. My marriage was destroying my life…while acting was saving my soul.

OSCAR
Sarah played Sardou's Russian princess, Fédora, with such tiger-ish passion and feline seduction, that no one has been able to equal it since.

SARAH
And if the newspapers hadn't been printing every tawdry detail of my bridal bed, you would have thought my life was perfection.

WILDE AND DIVINE – By Robert W. Cabell

OSCAR
(OSCAR walks to the bench.)
One of the things I loved about Sarah was she never talked about her problems–

SARAH
– a trick many people should learn.

OSCAR
I always tell my closest friends, 'Don't tell me about your problems, they're even more mundane than mine.' But now, poor Sarah–

SARAH
– like any damsel in distress–

OSCAR
– needed a hero–

SARAH
– and he appeared in the tumultuous form of–

OSCAR
– Jean Richepin. The only way to rid yourself of temptation is to surrender to it–

SARAH
– and Jean was very tempting–

OSCAR
– and surrender Sarah did.

SCENE V– LOVE'S LABORS LOST

SARAH
He was magnificent specimen–

OSCAR
– of healthy masculinity.

SARAH
With broad shoulders, an exuberant manner, and a warm, booming voice–

OSCAR
– as well as being a talented writer and poet.

SARAH
Jean had been a professional boxer–

OSCAR
– a stevedore–

SARAH
– a sharpshooter in the Franco-Prussian War, and then a sailor.

OSCAR
I just love a man... *out* of uniform.
(To the audience.)
And no, I am not gay – just mildly happy. And stop dirtying my mind with your innuendo. We are all in the gutter, but some of us are looking at the stars. You American's are obsessed with names, labels, and fads.
(He points to someone in the audience.)

OSCAR *(cont'd)*
'FADS' I said, not 'fags.' In America, if a gay man has "fruit" for lunch, he is either being redundant or done something illegal in seventeen states.
(Transitions back.)
Life is such a trial. Speaking of trials – let us not.
(Turns back to SARAH.)
Actually, if I had written *Sodom and Gomorrah* instead of *Salome*, I could have written the whole mess off as research.

SARAH
What a travesty it was. You were a sacrificial lamb on the altar of English hypocrisy.

OSCAR
I didn't do anything wrong.

SARAH
All of us, all of your friends, begged you to flee to Paris!

OSCAR
I did nothing wrong! I would not accept exile as an answer for freedom!

SARAH
No one would have thought less of you.

(SARAH turns upstage and becomes LADY WILDE.)

SCENE V– LOVE'S LABORS LOST

OSCAR
My family would. I would have been abandoning my wife and children, and my mother. She said,

SARAH *(as LADY WILDE)*
Oscar – I will always love you no matter what, and you will always be my son – as long as you don't run. You must stand and face whatever comes with honor.

OSCAR *(in the past)*
'I did nothing wrong.' *(OSCAR turns away in anger and defiance and faces upstage as SARAH crosses to him.)*

SARAH *(as LADY WILDE)*
(Touches him.) I know dear. And I was never so proud of you, my son, than when you stood before that court after they had sentenced you and said, 'The "love that dare not speak its name" in this century is such a great affection–'
(OSCAR, facing upstage, begins to say the words in unison with her.)

OSCAR *(in the past)* and **SARAH** *(as LADY WILDE)*
'–of an elder for a younger man as there was between David and Jonathan, such as Plato made as the very basis for his philosophy–'

(OSCAR slowly pivots around, facing the audience, taking over the speech as SARAH slowly moves around behind him and disappears.)

WILDE AND DIVINE – By Robert W. Cabell

OSCAR *(in the past – speaking alone)*
'– and such as you find in the sonnets of Michelangelo and Shakespeare. It is that deep, spiritual affection which is as pure as it is perfect. It dictates and pervades great works of art like those of Shakespeare and Michelangelo, and those two letters of mine, such as they are. It is in this century misunderstood, so much
misunderstood, that it may be described as the "love that dare not speak its name," and on account of it, I am placed where I am now.'
(Transition.)
It is beautiful, it is fine, it is the noblest form of affection. There is nothing unnatural about it. It is intellectual and it repeatedly exists between an elder and a younger man, when the elder man has intellect, and the younger man has all the joy, hope, and glamour of life before him. That it should be so, the world does not understand. The world mocks at it and sometimes puts one in the pillory for it.'

SARAH *(offstage as LADY WILDE)*
I love you, Oscar.

OSCAR
Mother died while I was in that god forsaken hell.
(SARAH steps forward and watches OSCAR cross.)
Constance came all the way to Reading Gaol to tell me, and they wouldn't even let her see me.

SCENE V– LOVE'S LABORS LOST

OSCAR

I was so alone, so desolated. And in the end, I went into self-imposed exile anyway.

SARAH

Like Victor Hugo. Both of you were *(reaches for him)* "great artists" and had more integrity than all the courts of law in the world put together!

OSCAR

I was never really free again – even in Paris and Italy. I was never really *me* again.

(SARAH crosses to him.)

SARAH

I am sorry I could not do more, be there more for you, Oscar. I was struggling to survive my own private hell.

OSCAR

We were both victims of our fancies for younger men. I wish I could have found a Jean Richepin for myself.

SARAH

I wish I could have valued him more than I did Jacques. Only five years separated Jean and me in age instead of the twelve years that separated me from Damala.

WILDE AND DIVINE – By Robert W. Cabell

OSCAR
(Aside to the audience.) Actually, age was never a barrier to Sarah – it was more like a boarding card.

SARAH
Jean Richepin was tremendously talented.

OSCAR
(Aside to audience.) And talent was something that never complicated Damala's life. The man was never afraid of failure – he did it too well.

SARAH
Richepin and I left Paris for a whirlwind tour of Europe–

OSCAR
– and each other! Sarah finally returned to Paris and to her senses.

SARAH
I legally separated from Damala and went on with my life, but as a Catholic, I could not get a divorce, which irritated Jean to no end.

OSCAR
But to her credit, Sarah stood by Damala during his last year and paid for his medical and personal bills as he dwindled and died from his drug addiction to morphine–

SCENE V– LOVE'S LABORS LOST

SARAH
– in 1889 at the age of thirty-four.

OSCAR
In life, it is our true friends and loved ones that are there for us through our personal travesties and tragedies. My beloved Constance was that kind of woman. Sarah was that kind of woman.
(Crosses downstage center.)
Beneath, beyond, behind – her pedestal – she took care of her mother, her sisters, her grandmother, her nieces, granddaughters, cousins, servants, and friends. Her son Maurice was always foremost in her concerns – with her lovers close behind. She was a woman of substance in the way that was as miraculous and divine – as her talent.

(The light goes out on OSCAR sitting quietly in his chair.)

SCENE VI

ALL ABOUT OSCAR

SARAH
You should understand one thing about Oscar; he became famous for being more quoted and published – a personality rather than an artist – long before he wrote anything of value or recognition. He toured America in 1882 and did not write his marvelous novel, *Dorian Grey*, until 1890, or his play, *Lady Windermere's Fan*, until 1892. *A Woman of No Importance* followed in 1893. *An Ideal Husband* and *The Importance of Being Earnest* both opened in 1896.
(SARAH crosses far downstage center into a spotlight as the rest of the stage goes black and OSCAR exits)
Oscar, from the moment he was born, was desperate to be "Oscar." He achieved it by posturing alongside the great celebrities and artists of his time and fiercely soliciting their friendships. Flattery will get you anywhere, and Oscar was the king of flattery – or a well-aimed snub! In fact, Oscar was named after the king of Sweden, who was also his godfather and a patient of his father, Lord William Wilde. Lord Wilde was also the royal physician to Queen Victory and two emperors, Maximilian of Mexico and Napoleon III.

(The lights slowly rise and the spot light fades allowing SARAH to move about the stage alone)

SCENE VI – ALL ABOUT OSCAR

SARAH
    The family lived in considerable style, and Oscar's mother, Lady Speranza, was a colorful personality and noted writer of classic Irish literature. In fact, Lady Wilde frequently went about London dressed as a high Druid Priestess, complete with flowing robes and elaborate, high head pieces, rings for each finger, and large ornate bracelets and broaches. She was also known for her well-attended "artistic" parties. She held them at her home twice a week, and her elder son, Willie – who was a noted critic and respected journalist for *Vanity Fair* (who Oscar would sometimes substitute for when Willie was away) – never failed to immortalize them in print.

(SARAH spreads her arms wide and shrugs, takes a beat, to decide to take the audience into her confidence and continues.)

    Speranza was a unique mother. Her husband, Dr. William Wilde, was quite the womanizer and had a dozen illegitimate children, with multiple ladies, who seemed to not bother or infringe upon her "rule of the roost." While Oscar was still young, his father grew very ill and soon passed away, and Speranza – as always – handled things in her own unique way.

(SARAH moves far downstage center to become LADY SPERANZA WILDE. OSCAR enter with a childish demeanor and speaks like a little boy.)

WILDE AND DIVINE – By Robert W. Cabell

OSCAR *(as a little boy)*
　Mama, who is that strange woman dressed in black with the veil that keeps coming here every day?

SARAH *(as LADY SPERANZA)*
　She is a "friend" of your father's.

OSCAR *(as a little boy)*
　Why does she sit by the bed all day long holding his hand?

SARAH *(as LADY SPERANZA)*
　Because it makes him happy, and he has very few days left to be happy – and it eases her pain.

OSCAR *(as a little boy)*
　But mother! People are talking. It doesn't seem very respectable. You are his wife.

SARAH *(as LADY SPERANZA)*
　Oscar? Do you know what the word respect means?

OSCAR *(as a little boy)*
　To honor and care for someone.

SARAH *(as LADY SPERANZA)*
　Who would you rather honor and care for – your father who is dying and finds great comfort in her presence, a woman your father has deep feelings for – or a crowd of small-minded gossips who are not your family or your friends?

SCENE VI – ALL ABOUT OSCAR

OSCAR *(as a little boy)*
My father, of course!

SARAH *(as LADY SPERANZA)*
Then let him have what he needs, and never, never use the word "respectable" in my house again! It is a word fit only for tradesmen.

(SARAH Laughs and returns to herself.)

SARAH
It was not the usual kind of family that one would think of in many ways, especially for a distinguished doctor. After having her first son, Willie, she had desperately wanted a daughter. So much so, that when Oscar was born, she dressed him up as a little girl until her next child was in fact, a girl. Isola Francesca was born when Oscar was five, and he adored her.

OSCAR
Sadly, little Isola died at the tender age of nine and left me hopelessly alone, again.

> Tread lightly, she is near
> Under the snow;
> Speak gently, she can hear
> The daisies grown.
> All her bright golden hair
> Tarnished with rust,
> She that was young and fair
> Fallen to dust.

OSCAR *(cont'd)*
>Coffin-board, heavy stone
>Lie on her breast,
>I vex my heart alone
>She is at rest.

>My older brother, Willie, was a boyish rogue who would grow up to be a man's man, and I – would not. We were joined by blood and duty, but not affection.

(OSCAR exits. (SARAH crosses to downstage left of the bench and the rest of the stage goes dark.)

SARAH
>When Oscar said, "Originality is no longer possible even in sin," he was quoting his writing, not his fashion sense. Oscar became famous for being infamous – both for his dazzling wit and his attire. He stood a few inches above six feet, and was never slim. He wore his hair in the 1870's to early 80's, quite long, and parted in the middle, flowing down on each side of his face and under his chin.
>He wore big hats, long velvet coats, and always sported a green neck tie and large bouquet-sized flowers like lilies or sunflowers flopping out of his button hole.

(She slowly crosses to downstage center as she continues.)
>One did not see Oscar in the morning or even early afternoon. He was constantly suffering from bottle fatigue! He was rather vampiristic in that he stayed up until dawn and slept most of the day.

SCENE VI – ALL ABOUT OSCAR

SARAH *(cont'd)*
He met France's greatest actor, Coquille, at my tea, and when Coquille invited him to join him for breakfast at his home one day at 9:00 am–

(OSCAR enters from behind the screen upstage right and crosses to downstage right of SARAH.)

OSCAR
– 9:00 in the morning? The man must be mad. I never stay up that late!

SARAH
Oscar met many great artists and writers at my daily court, which is why he liked them, in spite of my dogs. Oscar loathed dogs–

OSCAR
– nothing but four-footed forests for fleas!

SARAH
– which I love and have with me constantly. But he adored meeting Victor Hugo.

OSCAR
Hugo was so gracious, so kind, he sat and listened to me for hours without uttering a word!

WILDE AND DIVINE – By Robert W. Cabell

SARAH
Dear Victor was by then an octogenarian and slept through most of Oscar's conversation. He met Emile Zola, who did not like Oscar–

OSCAR
– nor in fact did John Singer Sargeant.

SARAH
It was odd that a man who immortalized the power and magic of painters in *Dorian Grey* was not liked by many painters. He had a huge falling out with Whistler–

OSCAR
– Whistler claimed I borrowed his ideas. Oh yes, let us put an old dowager in a chair in the middle of *The Importance of Being Ernest*, and let her rock all the way through the play! Why did I not think of that?

SARAH
And dear Audrey Beardsley always detested him.

OSCAR
Especially after I told the pretentious little git that he made a travesty of *Salome* with his savage and sadistic pictures. There was no beauty or poetry in his art. It was like a fabulous body with an unfortunate face.

SCENE VI – ALL ABOUT OSCAR

SARAH
And Degas was not found of Oscar either.

OSCAR
The man used far too much magenta in his art. Good God, what a painful color to look at. The very word "magenta" sounds malignant. It's from the family of ox-blood, only cheery! Would it not be lovely staring at ox-blood on the walls or having a lovely tea dress of that color – I think not!

SARAH
Oscar always seemed to get along with women much better than men. He was aesthetic, not athletic. If he fawned on you and you fawned back, it was devoted love. Then everything changed when Oscar met, fell in love with, and married Constance Lloyd.

OSCAR
'I am going to be married to a beautiful girl called Constance Lloyd. A grave, slight, violet-eyed little Artemis, with great coils of heavy brown hair and wonderful ivory hands, which draw music from the piano so sweet that the birds stop singing to listen to her.'

SARAH
Their wedding in London on May 29, 1884, packed the church, collected a large crowd outside, and had the appearance of a show. The Wilde's began their honeymoon by leaving at once for Paris.

WILDE AND DIVINE – By Robert W. Cabell

OSCAR

I took Constance to see Sarah in *Macbeth*, the most splendid acting I ever saw. She simply stormed the part! I think Constance learned to understand why Paris was my favorite city in the world. While we were there, we were treated like royalty. It was like a fairy tale romance. So, we returned to London in high spirits and took up residence in a charming house on Tite Street, in Chelsea.

SARAH

We all seem to love to hold our own little courts and keep our loved ones and disciples close at hand to absorb the energy of adoration, and Oscar sucked it up like a kitten at a saucer of milk. He threw a lovely soiree for me in their home one night and had me stand on the table to sign his ceiling – which became a quirky little tradition for him and his more celebrated friends. Soon, Oscar was dressing up his shy little Constance and having "at homes," which became all the rage.

OSCAR

Everyone in London wanted to be invited to a Wilde party.

(SARAH takes on the role of CONSTANCE.)

SCENE VI – ALL ABOUT OSCAR

SARAH *(as CONSTANCE)*
Oscar! This is getting out of control! Mr. Houdini is hanging by his heels from the chandelier getting out of Willie's handcuffs, Whistler is shouting at Mr. Beerbohm over his last review, and your mother is at it again.

OSCAR *(in the past)*
What has mother done?

SARAH *(as CONSTANCE)*
She's wearing her Druid robes again – and Sarah showed up between matinees in her Joan of Arc costume, and this is the third time Count Montesquieu has arrived as Salome since you started writing it. Now Ellen Terry and Mrs. Campbell are both rummaging through our wardrobe to create makeshift costumes, while Beardsley is madly sketching the whole thing on my linen tablecloth – which Mr. Kean is standing on to sign the ceiling for the third time! And to top it all off, Oscar, no one – and I mean no one – has figured out that you dressed me as Queen Elizabeth. Really Oscar! Next time, I want to wear the Titania outfit and you can wear one of your togas.

(SARAH and OSACR both laugh again as themselves and OSCAR looks at audience.)

WILDE AND DIVINE – By Robert W. Cabell

OSCAR
Poor, dear, Constance – she was lovely–

SARAH
– but a bit dull.

OSCAR
No– just totally out of her depth when it came to my artistic circle of friends. *(OSCAR shakes his head and chuckles to himself.)*

SARAH
(Aside to the audience.) I remember when she came crying to me after the whole homosexual escapade hit the papers and asked me why Oscar could love Lord Douglass and not her? "What does he have that I haven't got?" she asked. *(She lifts an eyebrow and sighs.)* No! I did not find it necessary to enlighten her!

(Lights go to black.)

SCENE VII

SAINTS AND SINNERS

(Lights rise on OSCAR alone on stage.)

OSCAR
    Yes, 1890 was a great year for me – and another of many for Sarah. In 1890, Sarah toured London, and her fans followed her with cultist frenzy –
(A blue light rises on SARAH as she enters and curtseys like a curtain call, waving and nodding to her fans.)
    – devouring each new photo, paying fortunes for dried up flowers, snips of her hair, and soiled handkerchiefs – any bits or pieces of personal items her maids and stagehands were entrepreneurial enough to pass off and sell outside the stage door. But sweet Sarah specialized in the portrayal, however so delicate, of fallen or wanton women. Many a proper English mother longed for her to portray a role they could take their young daughters to see. Sarah, being a mother and the good French girl that she was, decided to storm London in 1890 with the saintly visage of *Jeanne d'Arc* in Jules Barbier's play.

(SARAH steps out of her hooded robe and is wearing a Joan of Arc outfit.)

SARAH
    At forty-six, both a widow and a grandmother–

WILDE AND DIVINE – By Robert W. Cabell

OSCAR
– her dazzling portrayal of a nineteen-year-old maid–

SARAH
– persecuted by the English priests, burned at the stake as a witch for leading her people in holy insurrection–

OSCAR
– conquered the hearts of London.

SARAH
(SARAH smiles at OSCAR and steps forward ready to act.) Viva la France!

(OSCAR takes on the character of BISHOP LOYSELEUR and SARAH becomes JEANNE D'ARC.)

          BISHOP LOYSELEUR
The crime is evident – the sentence! – haste – we've no time to waste.

          JEANNE D'ARC
My death will bring no fortune to your side, for were you tens of thousands – to abide in France for more than seven short years at most will bring destruction on you and your host.

SCENE VII – SAINTS AND SINNERS

BISHOP LOYSELEUR
You lie! That is a vain boast! Your king is but a dunce. You know your fate?

JEANNE D' ARC
(Rises high on her knees.) I see it.

BISHOP LOYSELEUR
Then God must hate us?

JEANNE D' ARC
(Rises to her feet.) God hates no one! *(Points accusingly.)* Kneel before his throne, for mercy, make appeal.

BISHOP LOYSELEUR
You love to see the blood of Christians flow.

JEANNE D' ARC
To that my life and actions answer, no! The very dead will rise, the deeds to tell 'neath my standard. Ah, you know them well.

BISHOP LOYSELEUR
Confess that you a wicked sorceress are, and that a magic banner led the war!

WILDE AND DIVINE – By Robert W. Cabell

JEANNE D' ARC
(SARAH raises her hand in protest.) 'Tis false. I never used nor spells nor charms, to give unlawful victory to my arms. When you were massed to do your very worst, my men rushed in and I among the first. A nobler prince there walks not on this earth. If fault there be 'tis mine. I know his worth.

BISHOP LOYSELEUR
Where did you get your courage?

JEANNE D' ARC
From my God.

BISHOP LOYSELEUR
Becomes you then to bow beneath the rod. Your king is but a heretic, and I condemn him as a bastard.

JEANNE D' ARC
Sir! You lie!

BISHOP LOYSELEUR
Since this abandoned culprit still doth hurl defiance to all voices save the fiends, who she avers are saints, and on them leans, denies the "Unum Sanctum" of our creed *(Walks around her.)*…

SCENE VII – SAINTS AND SINNERS

BISHOP LOYSELEUR *(cont'd)*
the church which cannot countenance a deed of blood herself, the secular arm now calls to do her justice.

JEANNE D' ARC
The stake! Ah, my courage fails, I tremble and my wonted color pales. Must this poor body this in flames expire? Give me another death, I am afraid, God will not torture thus a helpless maid. *(She pauses to gain courage and resolution, and rises.)*
At least, if in the fire I now must die, give me my god – *(makes the sign of the cross on her chest)* my soul…to fortify.

(OSCAR releases the character of BISHOP LOYSELEUR.)

OSCAR
Though her portrayal of *Jeanne d'Arc* was triumphant, the play itself was lackluster. It is sad, but, "All bad art begins with good intentions." Luckily, Sardou continued to write brilliant roles of fallen women for her to play. Oddly enough, the male roles she chose were tortured and saintly, like her Hamlet. In fact, Bernhardt was the first woman to ever triumph in the part of Hamlet and the only woman to triumph in both the roles of Hamlet and Ophelia.
(Crosses downstage left to the bench.)
Her Hamlet haunted and mesmerized all of France, England, and America – but it was in 1896 that she took her greatest venture into the male psyche–

WILDE AND DIVINE – By Robert W. Cabell

(SARAH crosses behind the dressing screen and takes off the white tunic with the red cross of JEANNE D'ARC and dons a long brown, velvet, man's tunic heavily embroidered, as OSCAR continues.)

OSCAR *(cont'd)*
– when she played Lorenzaccacio, the ambivalent Brutus of Florence, a young nobleman who assassinated his best friend, the tyrannical Duke of Florence, on a bet.

(SARAH takes on the character of LORENZACCACIO.)

LORENZACCACIO
Oh, you're a good man, Filippo, you have led a virtuous life. But you have seen only the surface while I have explored the depths. The fault of books and historians is that they depict men differently from what they are. A man can live in a city all his life and see only the parks and the palaces, but what does he know if he never enters the brothels and the gambling dens? If you are concerned for your fellow man and you want to do something for humanity, you are a fool! Because it won't be long before you discover you stand alone.

(LORENZACCACIO crosses downstage left in a boastful manner speaking to the crowd.)

SCENE VII – SAINTS AND SINNERS

LORENZACCACIO *(cont'd)*
I am Lorenzaccacio. Have you seen me as I walk through the streets of this city? The children don't throw mud at me. No one slips poison into my cup. The beds of young girls are still wet from my sweat and yet their fathers do not attack me as I leave. In return for a few miserable pieces of gold, a loving mother will offer her daughter to me. And, when I smile, it is just to suffocate a scream inside.
(Takes a moment to shake off the shame.)
I could have cried for the first virgin that I abused until that moment when she began to laugh, Filippo. I had barely taken the first step of my journey when I saw that everyone was doing the same as I was doing. The whole of society lifted its veil to show me a price stamped on its forehead. I saw men as they a really are. And I asked myself, 'Who am I doing this for?'
(Moves across the stage as if walking through the city.)
I would go for a walk around the streets of Florence, look at a stranger, and ask myself, 'When I have done this act, will he benefit by it?' I watched the republicans in their studies, I visited the shops, I listened to people talking, I saw the effect of Tyranny upon them.
(Turns to confront his friend.)

LORENZACCACIO *(cont'd)*
I was always looking, waiting, waiting for humanity to show me one honest face. I will take a bet with you, Filippo. I am going to kill Allesandro. Once he is dead anything will be possible. The republicans can take power if they act as they should. I bet, Filippo, that nobody does a thing!

SCENE VIII

SALOME

OSCAR

One of my greatest creations, which I poured my soul into, was *Salome*. I could never envision anyone but Sarah as my Salome. In fact, I wrote the original text in French – and Sarah consented to star in and produce the production.

SARAH

I think Oscar personally identified with the besotted, hedonistic Herod. I certainly identified with Salome. There were several people I could think of whose head I wanted on a silver platter.

OSCAR

But *Salome* was to be my greatest disappointment. We were in rehearsals – the sets and costumes, meticulously supervised by Sarah herself, were under construction – when the Lord Chamberlain of Censorship informed us that the laws forbid any productions of Biblical characters.

(SARAH looks at OSCAR, and she walks off stage sadly and a little annoyed.)

I laughed at first and thought, this is Sarah Bernhardt! Of course the Prince of Wales will intervene. He was one of Sarah's best friends. He would sometimes slip backstage in London and play an extra in one of her

WILDE AND DIVINE – By Robert W. Cabell

OSCAR *(cont'd)*
performances. He owned several of her paintings. His wife, Princess Alexandria, was devoted to Sarah. But he did not – or rather could not – budge the queen or the law, and the production was abandoned in midstream. It put a heavy strain on my friendship with Sarah. She was always pleasant and kind to me, but it was never quite the same after that. Once again, I was never quite the same.

(OSCAR sits down.)
I was a man who stood in symbolic relationship to the art and culture of my age... the gods had given me almost everything. I had genius, a distinguished name, high social position, brilliancy, intellectual daring. I made art a philosophy, and philosophy an art. I altered the minds of men and the color of things. There was nothing I said or did that did not make people wonder. I treated art as the supreme reality and life as a mere mode of fiction. I awoke the imagination of my century so that it created myth and legend around me. I summed up all systems in a phrase, and all existence in an epigram.

(OSCAR rises and exits, saddened.)

SCENE IX

I LOVE PARIS

(A few years later.)

(In The BLACKNESS there is the tolling of a bell striking midnight. As it strikes for the ninth time, it begins to cross-fade to the sound of a ticking clock. The lights rise very slowly as the clock sound fades and SARAH enters wearing her dressing robe with her hair in a tight French twist.)

SARAH
It was but a few years ago I stood on this very same stage with my dear friend Oscar, sharing our triumphs and our sorrows. So much has changed since then. His great light has gone out, and all the world is darker for it. *(Smiles softly)* Oscar and I shared several things. The love of handsome young men was only one of them. We both had Dutch ancestry, me through my mother and Oscar by his grandfather. We both loved Paris to distraction and both worshiped Napoleon.
(Laughs.)
Oscar said that Napoleon was the greatest success story and the greatest failure in history. So it was fitting that the last thing he ever saw me do, just before he died, was *L'Aiglon*–
(SARAH steps out of her robe and is wearing a man's white military uniform.)

WILDE AND DIVINE – By Robert W. Cabell

SARAH *(cont'd)*
– Edmond Rostand's illuminating classic on the life and failure of Napoleon's nineteen-year-old son, the Duke of Reichstadt. He struggled to regain his father's throne and rule his time. Though he failed as Oscar failed, both were raised back upon a literary throne, and I – I always dedicated this part of my performance to him.

(SARAH *as the DUKE)*

DUKE

To reign! I mount and ride to reign! But first, Wargram, I let thy strong wind bear me up, thy breath of glory slake my lifelong thirst. Here of thy air I drink the stirrup-cup! To reign! Not like those old safe, stupid kings. How tired they must become of life at court. But to reign, to serve high causes, do great things. Right wrong – ah – Prokesch, that is noble sport.

(Makes a sweeping gesture to the crowd.)

People who wrote the legend with your blood, come welcome home at last the Emperor's son. He will repay, in peace, all things good the glory that you lent Napoleon.

(Strikes a defiant pose)

Hence forth we will fight only for the right; our wars of conquest shall from this day cease. I seem to see a mother, through

DUKE *(cont'd)*
the night hold her child and call on me for peace. Oh France, I have suffered too much not to hear; I have fed too much on falsehoods to be false. Liberty, liberty, you need not fear a prince who has lived his life in prison walls. *(Shakes fists defiantly in the air.)* I will – I will – O, I am going to reign! I am twenty! Youth and my expectancy bear me upon their wings beyond this plain to where my capital is waiting for me. *(DUKE sees the sweeping vista in his mind.)* O perfume of the chestnut trees along the way that I shall ride! O flags that burn, three colored in the sun! O drunken throng! O the return, the glorious return! The great, fierce city hails me as I go! The people cheer and sing, the children dance, muskets are brandished. To be welcomed so by Paris is to kiss the lips of France.

(SARAH holds the final moment as if reluctant to let it pass, and then releases the character and bites back tears that come from another place.)

SARAH
Oscar, as France's official Ambassadress of Goodwill – as the lips of France – I kiss you. I adore you, and I will always miss and remember you!

END OF SHOW

SARAH BERNHARDT
HER ROLES, MENTORS AND MEN

Sarah as The Little Queen

SARAH BERNHARDT
HER ROLES, MENTORS AND MEN

Sarah as Dona Sol

SARAH BERNHARDT
HER ROLES, MENTORS AND MEN

Sarah as Pheadra

SARAH BERNHARDT
HER ROLES, MENTORS AND MEN

Sarah as Marguerite

SARAH BERNHARDT
HER ROLES, MENTORS AND MEN

Sarah as Tosca

SARAH BERNHARDT
HER ROLES, MENTORS AND MEN

Sarah as Hamlet

SARAH BERNHARDT
HER ROLES, MENTORS AND MEN

Sarah as Lorenzaccio

SARAH BERNHARDT
HER ROLES, MENTORS AND MEN

Sarah as Jeanne de Arc

SARAH BERNHARDT
HER ROLES, MENTORS AND MEN

Sarah as the Duke

SARAH BERNHARDT
HER ROLES, MENTORS AND MEN

Sarah's son Maurice Bernhardt

SARAH BERNHARDT
HER ROLES, MENTORS AND MEN

Mounet Sulley, Sarah's first Leading man and lover

SARAH BERNHARDT
HER ROLES, MENTORS AND MEN

Jacques Damala the only husband of Sarah

SARAH BERNHARDT
HER ROLES, MENTORS AND MEN

Jean Richepin Leading man and lover

SARAH BERNHARDT
HER ROLES, MENTORS AND MEN

Sarah and her granddaughter Lysiane

SARAH BERNHARDT
HER ROLES, MENTORS AND MEN

Victor Hugo
Author and Mentor

SARAH BERNHARDT
HER ROLES, MENTORS AND MEN

Victorien Sardou
Author and Mentor

OSCAR WILDE
FRIENDS AND FAMILY

Young Oscar Wilde

OSCAR WILDE
FRIENDS AND FAMILY

Young Oscar Wilde

OSCAR WILDE
FRIENDS AND FAMILY

Young Oscar Wilde

OSCAR WILDE
FRIENDS AND FAMILY

Lady Speranza Wilde

OSCAR WILDE
FRIENDS AND FAMILY

Constance Wilde and son Cyril

OSCAR WILDE
FRIENDS AND FAMILY

Cyril and Vivian Wilde with unknown man.

OSCAR WILDE
FRIENDS AND FAMILY

Willie Wilde, Oscars older brother

OSCAR WILDE
FRIENDS AND FAMILY

Oscar Wilde and Lord Alfred Douglas

OSCAR WILDE
FRIENDS AND FAMILY

Lord Alfred Douglas and his brother Francis

OSCAR WILDE
FRIENDS AND FAMILY

Oscar dressed as Salome

THE DIVINE GOLDEN YEARS

PART III OF THE DIVINE TRILOGY OF SARAH BERNHARDT

THE LIFE AND TIMES OF SARAH BERNHARDT

A Play Robert W. Cabell

Original Score by Keith Kemper

Directed by Peter McLean

A One Woman Show
as Performed by Louise Martin

THE DIVINE GOLDEN YEARS

Produced in reparatory at:

The Trilogy Theater
341 West 44thStreet
New York, NY 10036
In 2001

No part of this script may be used or reproduced by any means, graphic, electronic, or mechanical: including photocopying, recording, taping, or by any information storage retrieval system, without the written permission of the publisher, except in the case of brief quotations embodied in critical articles and reviews.

THE DIVINE GOLDEN YEARS

is dedicated to
my parents, Rudy and Jackie, who have
celebrated over sixty years of marriage
and are still going strong together
in their golden years.

CHARACTER

SARAH BERNHARDT: The mother of Sarah Bernhardt, her aunt, and two sisters were all known for their great beauty and were celebrated courtesans of Paris. Sarah herself was considered thin and plain, but with an exceptionally rich and melodious speaking voice. Her reddish-blonde hair was thick, frizzy, and unruly, her arms overly long, her bust too small, and her nose too big. Yet when she walked onstage in the character of one of her fallen women, she imbued herself with a radiance and internal war of emotions that transformed her into the pinnacle of style and sensuality. She was the first woman to successfully portray the male role of Hamlet, and the only actress to receive rave reviews for both the roles of Hamlet and Ophelia.

    Bernhardt embraced a personal life that was equally daring and dramatic. She slept in a coffin, traveled with a menagerie of wild and exotic animals, including panthers, rhinos and pythons, was the first woman to ride in a hot air balloon, hunted bears and crocodiles, and had a love of all things strange and macabre. Her onstage love scenes were equally matched by her torrid affairs, well into her 70's. Most of her leading men were her lovers, and her closest personal friend was a notorious lesbian. That combined with her sold out, salacious performances, made her the most famous woman in the world for over half a century.

    Sarah was anti-drugs, anti-smoking, and vehemently against the death penalty in an era when civilization accepted all of those. Her circle of intimate friends included the greatest writers of her time, like Oscar Wilde, Alexander Dumas, Victor Hugo, Mark Twain, and royalty such as, Edward the Prince of Wales and his wife Princess Alexandra. The Czar of Russia knelt to her, a Belgium prince fathered her only child, and the Grand Duke of Austria vacated his castle for her use. President Teddy Roosevelt was a devoted fan, as well as some of the greatest intellectuals of her time such as, Edison, Tesla, and Freud.

At fifty she was convincingly portraying nineteen year old virgins, and her romantic scenes were both the rage and scandal of the civilized world. Dying on stage slowly, tortuously, languidly, and tragically, was her greatest specialty.

Those who came after her desperately tried to mimic her poses and gestures which were organic to her unique talents. Those who mimicked her were judged as overly dramatic or cliché. No audience that saw Bernhardt "die," escaped the onslaught of the deep and overwhelming emotions she conveyed.

SETTING

The set has three basic areas. Down stage left is a gilded French vanity with a gold framed mirror on the vanity which is scattered with bottles and boxes and jewelry, with a silver brush and comb set. Stage left of the vanity is an exotic looking full length carved tri-folding mirror. It has inset panels of fur, and shells inset in various patterns around the recessed mirrors.

On the upstage right side of the vanity (no more than two or three steps away), is an elegant and lavishly dressing screen decorated with Sarah's theatrical posters designed by Muca with some of her greatest roles. Draped over the edges of the dressing screen are a Kimono, a hooded floor-length velvet cape, and various, shawls, scarves and gloves. Hooked on top to the far stage right side of the screen are two or three hats of various sizes. Directly in front of the dressing screen to one side is a large brass umbrella stand. Inside are parasols, a sword and scabbard, and an African death stick from New Orleans,(a tall wooden staff with a carved human skull on top.)

Upstage center is a divan, or fainting couch draped in red brocade. Various sizes of pots and vases full of flowers are on either side of the divan both on the floor and on top of stacks of books and baskets. Two mismatched elegant side tables with picture frames, and crystal decanters frame the divan. On a silver tray is a crystal goblet, that Sarah will fill and drink from the decanters throughout the show. This is an essential element for the actress to keep her voice in shape and should be worked into the staging of the show.

The wall has gilded framed theatrical posters and paintings of Sarah, and collections of masks and artifacts from many different countries and cultures. In front of the Divan is a battered wooden traveling chest, with a leopard skin fur shawl draped to one side. The other side has a large brass hand fan with peacock feathers. Throughout the show Sarah will, take things from the trunk, sit or even stand up on it.

Far down stage right is an open space that is framed in front by a half circle of brass antique foot lights. Far upstage and directly behind this open area is a white scrim, framed across the top and draped to the floor on either side by classic style dark red velvet drapes. It gives the effect of a small proscenium arch and when Sarah recreates most of her famous monologues they will begin or end in this space. The white scrim area is used for projections of clouds during the hot air balloon monologues and projections of the images of war.

COSTUMES

Sarah wears a long simple full length sleeveless white sheath with a long white trailing silk scarf around her neck thrown backwards across each shoulder trailing to the floor.

During the show she will use it as a shawl or a to tie and wrap and drape her dress in several different styles. Around her neck she wears a gold locket on a chain that never comes off. The use of various accessories such as hats, gloves, robes, kimono and wigs, and jewelry will also be added and discarded as the show progresses.

THE DIVINE GOLDEN YEARS

A Play by Robert W. Cabell

SCENE I

THE REBIRTH OF PARIS

(The lights rise on a red divan with a lithe prone feline body in a shimmering long Angel-white gown. We hear the sound of voices murmuring prayers in Latin and soft hovering strings)

SARAH

I am Madame Sarah Bernhardt, and I am dying. At the age of seventy-nine, I am dying. My son Maurice has covered my unconscious body with wildflowers, and the priest has said the last rights as my body stubbornly clings to its last few breaths and the crowds of loving and loyal Parisians encircle my house.
(She rises from the divan with a sultry laugh.)
Dear God what a life I have led. And quand même, in spite of everything, I have few if any true regrets.
(Points straight out above the heads of the audience.)
As you die, they say your whole life passes before you.
(Looks around at the audience and smiles.)
And, I suppose, that is what is happening to me now. My early life flickers past quickly. No secrets.
(Shrugs matter-of-factly.)
The world knows I was the illegitimate daughter of a Dutch courtesan. They know my son was also born out of wedlock—fathered by a Belgian prince. So what! Lily Langtry had a child by the Prince of Wales. I was just, as you say, "keeping up with the Jones'!"

THE DIVINE GOLDEN YEARS – *by Robert W. Cabell*

SARAH

Lilly and I actually had several things in common. Both acclaimed actresses, both had an illegitimate child by a prince, neither of us wore corsets, both adored Oscar Wilde, both of us toured America, and we even posed together for a postcard. Which, to my everlasting chagrin, she was paid more for than I!

But it was I, by the age of thirty-six, who had conquered the hearts of England, France, and North America to become the world's greatest actress. But there is so much more.

Let me share with you my memories with what little time I have left, as I cling here between Heaven and Hell. *(Laughs.)* The vote will be close on that one!

Right now I am remembering my return to Paris from my first American Tour. I was to make seven more tours of that vast country before I lay here dying.

On the day we were to arrive, I was so anxious to see my son, I spent the afternoon practicing how I would greet him: 'My Son! My child! It has been such torture to be apart from you! ... Ah Maurice, how can I tell you how much, how desperately, how terribly, I have missed you? ... Mama is home my darling, and with an ache of longing that can only be satiated by the sight of her own little man!'

I spent less time preparing for Lady Macbeth.

SCENE I - THE REBIRTH OF PARIS

SARAH

My first American tour lasted six grueling months through fifty-two cites, and I returned with a pot of gold and a resolve to spend more time with my son.

His youth, like mine, was spent too much in the company of nurses and nannies, while I was off on tour... much like my mother left me while she was off with her lords and lovers. But where Mama was dutiful but distant, Maurice and I adored each other! I was magical and ethereal to him. I lavished him with princely treasures and he accepted them as naturally as a breath of air. When I returned from America, he took his place by my side. He shared the fantasy of my admirers who called me a goddess, "the Divine Sarah," as my friend Oscar Wilde dubbed me, and soon had all of England and France calling me the same.

It is not easy to live up to such adoration. I never wanted to disappoint my son. I never let my Maurice see me cry. He never saw me out of makeup, or weary and tired. You must never tarnish a myth. The Golden Fleece is ever enchanting. Woolen nightgowns, cold crème, and hairnets create nothing but nightmares and indigestion.

So, in a way, America brought my son and me closer together. But my first tour of America did not make me popular at home in France. They thought it was an insult to Racine and Moliere to perform such literary treasures before vulgar Yankee millionaires, illiterate cowboys, and blanketed Indians. Nonsense!

THE DIVINE GOLDEN YEARS – *by Robert W. Cabell*

SARAH
> I considered myself an ambassadress of goodwill and culture—and a very well paid ambassadress at that! But Paris thought otherwise, largely due to the slanders and lies of my one-time friend, Marie Colombier. She had written all sorts of heinous serial stories, claiming the tour, which she herself was in, was a calamitous string of horrendous flops, and that I was a has-been!
>
> Nothing could have been further from the truth! But, I won back the hearts of Paris by waylaying a long time friend and colleague of mine. I had her maid, my accomplice, rush into her garden.

(Sarah snatches up an ornate peacock feather fan and pretends to dust with it like a maid.)

SARAH *(as the maid)*
> Oh, Madame Agar, I have such terrible news! Your handsome Captain, he—he— *(Sobs.)*

SARAH
> She had a tendency to overact—badly.

SARAH *(as the maid)*
> *(Sobs some more.)* The poor man has had an accident! He is being taken to surgery this very moment. They say he may die!

(SARAH regains her composure and laughs.)
> This sent Agar fleeing to his side, out of town. . .

(SARAH makes a sweeping gesture with the feathered fan and then waves goodbye with it, and suddenly laughs.)

SCENE I - THE REBIRTH OF PARIS

SARAH
(She brings the fan back to use as a regular fan in a coquettish manner.)
> Of course, it was mere hours before a grand gala. Oh yes, and it was truly grand!

(She tosses the fan unceremoniously down on to a pillow.)
> It was for the crème de la crème of Paris. And "she," which would now be "me," was to be the grand finale!

(SARAH glides dramatically downstage center in to a spotlight as the stage dims around her.)

> You have never seen two thousand faces turn white and gasp with amazement like they did that night. Eyes flew wide when I strode center stage unannounced to seize the climatic moment. With the mere power of my voice and the tenacity of my presence, I won them back. Merely reciting a few lines of verse to an orchestral swell, I whipped them into a patriotic frenzy!

> The Gods of theater were with me that night like they never were before! It was a miraculous onslaught of audacity that swept all derision and doubt of my talent aside and made me the reigning muse of Paris once more.

(SARAH bows deeply as the lights rise and then looks at the audience suddenly and winks.)

> And my friend, my dear Agar, found the whole escapade clever and amusing and completely forgave my sly deception.

THE DIVINE GOLDEN YEARS – *by Robert W. Cabell*

SARAH
(SARAH saunters upstage right to sit at her dressing table.)
The Vaudeville Theater's manager, Deslandes, and the playwright, the formidable Victorien Sardou, were once again desperate for me to perform the lead in a new play called *Fedora*. However, I did not wish to forget the way they had slighted me so rudely upon my return from America. Just like a wayward suitor returned to his lady-love, I wanted to be courted—no—I wanted them to crawl.

(SARAH jumps up from her stool and stamps her foot like a petulant child.)

How dare they! How dare everybody treat me like some no-talent-has-been after my international triumph! They banished me based on the lies of the two faced whore, Marie Colombier. Actually I shouldn't say that, because if she had another face, she'd use it. That twisted, conniving little... Oh well... one would think after forty more years of living well—the best revenge they say—and her fading off into oblivion, I would have gotten past all that. My dears, in life you must always forgive, but never, *never* forget!

(SARAH sits again and composers herself and applies some makeup, dabs on some perfume on and slips a piece of jewelry on.)
But let's flicker past that to more pleasant memories. Ah, yes, Sardou and *Fedora*. This was to be the beginning of what would be my most successful professional collaboration.

SCENE I - THE REBIRTH OF PARIS

SARAH
(SARAH rises and crosses stage center in front of the divan as she speaks.)
Sarah and Sardou" would become a byword for theatrical spectaculars: *Fedora, Theodora, Tosca, Cleopatra,* and *Grismonda and Le Sorcier.* But at that time, I kept my interest in check and invited Deslandes *(SARAH sits on her divan grandly as if waiting to be entertained..)* and Sardou to present me the script in my garden, which was really more like a jungle of flowers, vines, and potted flora. Sardou explained to me…

SARAH *(as Sardou deepens her voice)*
Fedora is the drama of a rebel and a Russian princess. The Princess Fedora is duped into believing a handsome nihilist named Loris Ipanoff assassinated her husband. She plots with the secret police to ensnare his heart with her amorous charms and deliver him into their hands.

SARAH
Poor Sardou; he was an instinctive director, always puffing and strutting about as he read a script, performing and gesticulating for every role. He continued,

SARAH *(as Sardou)*
As the play unfolds, Fedora falls madly in love with Loris, who turns out to be neither a revolutionary nor the assassin of who she discovers was an unfaithful husband.

THE DIVINE GOLDEN YEARS – *by Robert W. Cabell*

SARAH
He tripped over a rose bush, trounced on a section of my herbaceous border, and shattered a lovely porcelain jardinière of lavender and jasmine.

SARAH *(as Sardou)*
Rather than fulfill her contract with the secret police and reveal her treachery, she takes poison and dies in the arms of her lover.

SARAH
It was the last throws of the death scene that claimed my poor lovely jardinière, but what a death scene! When Loris cries for help after Fedora takes her poison…

(She jumps up and dramatically pantomimes draining a vial of deadly poison.)

SARAH *(as Fedora)*

It is useless Loris. It is deadly beyond remedy. I have not five minutes to live.
(She collapses back down onto the divan.)
Leave me alone I pray you out of charity.
(She supports herself with one hand holding on to the back of the divan and one outstretched to ward him off.)
No Loris! It is all over and it is better so. You will pardon me dead. If I were living there would always be those phantoms between us to separate us. It is better I should go.

SCENE I - THE REBIRTH OF PARIS

SARAH *(as Fedora)*

(She doubles up in agony and falls onto the floor.)
    Oh God! What agony! It is burning me. Water! Water! OH!
(She slumps to the floor.)
    I am cold, so cold. Take me in your arms Loris. I could wish for yet a little of your love, and then to rest upon your heart, the long sleep coming.
(She goes blind.)
    Loris, Loris! Where are you? Your hands, give me your hands and your lips, your adored lips that I may leave my soul.

SARAH
(She looks at the audience and smiles.)
    And she dies upon a kiss. *(laughs and rise to her feet)* Sardou and I shared the same unerring instinct for theater and I knew this would be a triumph.

And, I knew that Deslandes' offer of 1,000 francs a performance for a guaranteed 100 performances was a very fine contract, but then came my time for revenge.

I smiled like a little coquette and said he should not tease me. He looked confused. I was sweet. I was charming. And I was completely resolute when I explained that the Vaudeville could make 7500 francs a performance, and I wanted 1500 of that, plus 25% of the net profits, or sadly, as much as I loved M. Sardou's new play, I could not accept.

THE DIVINE GOLDEN YEARS – *by Robert W. Cabell*

SARAH
Deslandes was pale as a ghost and decimated by my resolution, but he acquiesced. I would begin my rehearsals when I returned to Paris after my European tour.

SCENE II

TO RUSSIA WITH LOVE

SARAH
(She crosses grandly stage right as she takes her earings off and drops them on her dressing table.)

When I announced my European Tour, I refused any and all bookings in Germany. After what they did to France during the Siege of Paris, I would not dirty my hands with their despicable money. They sent a delegation to beg me. They claimed they would pay anything! I could name my price!

So, I turned to them and smiled deliciously, and wet my lips with anticipation to make them hush and lean forward to hear what number I would contrive for my fee. What was the price of Sarah Bernhardt's pride? Eh? I drew myself up regally, and in my haughtiest voice cried, 'My price is two hundred million francs…

(Laughs haughtily.)

…which was the "price of peace" Bismarck demanded France pay to Germany for the war of 1870.' The delegation turned pale and hastily departed.

For luck, we began the tour in London at the Gaiety, and for the first time the ban on censorship of *La Dame Aux Camélias* by Alexander Dumas, was lifted in my honor, though not without great trepidation and coaxing by Prince Edward.

(She sits casually on the edge of the divan.)

THE DIVINE GOLDEN YEARS – *by Robert W. Cabell*

SARAH
He explained to Victoria that I played Marguerite with such fragile intensity and delicate sensuality, that she herself eventually attended a performance.

(She partially reclines on the divan.)

To me the most touching moment for Marguerite was the moment in the last scene, right after she realizes even with Armand's return and the letter of acceptance from his father, there will be no miraculous cure, not even an extra hour of life for her. So, she says to him tenderly as she feels death kneeling beside her:

SARAH *(as Marguerite)*

Armand, go to my dressing table. In a box you will find a locket. It is my portrait, in the days when I was pretty! I had it made for you; keep it. It will help you remember me later on. But, if one day you are loved by a pure, young girl and you marry her, as it must be, and as I wish it to be, and if she finds this portrait, tell her that it is of a friend who, if God allows her to do so from some obscure little corner in Heaven, prays every day for her and for you. If she is jealous of the past, as we so often are, we women, if she asks of you the sacrifice of this portrait, make it without fear, without remorse; it will be right, and I forgive you in advance.

(SARAH releases the character of Marguerite, and sits up.)

SCENE II - TO RUSSIA WITH LOVE

SARAH
From England we played middle France, then Northern Italy, where King Umberto gifted me with a glorious hand painted eighteenth century Venetian fan, which could only be surpassed by the priceless parure of rare cameos Franz Joseph bequest to me in honor of my Phaedra.

We played Belgium, Switzerland, and Holland, where I was truly treated like royalty. But it was in Austria where the Archduke Frederic put one of his own palaces at my disposal, saying that no hotel was a fit residence for a "queen."

(SARAH rises and strides forward.)

The tour was beyond triumphant as we swept into Russia. Odessa was the only blemish. The Russians in Odessa are extremely anti-Semitic. You must understand that in Europe they do not consider Judaism a religion, but a race.

I was raised as a Catholic and am devoutly religious, and I am only one quarter Jewish through my maternal grandmother, but I will always be called a Jew.

I refuse to be ashamed of anything I am, and I hate racism in any form. It is cowardly and stupid! This was never stated more eloquently than in Sardou's *La Sorciere*, when Zoraya, a Moorish woman in the 1500's, is brought before the Inquisition for her heathen faith.

THE DIVINE GOLDEN YEARS – *by Robert W. Cabell*

SARAH *(as Zoraya)*

(She leaps up on top of the trunk.)

I dare anything, now! At least I will have the joy of crying my loathing at this tribunal of priests. Ay, my hatred! I hate you! Priests who hasten upon a conquered people like jackals after a battle. Of all the suffering of the vanquished there's not one we have not known. You have made your churches out of our Mosques.

You have kenneled your dogs in our courts of justice. You have stalled your horses in our schools. You have broken our canals, polluted our ponds, burned our mills. Our orchards have been cut down and all Granada is a dessert, but this was not enough!

We were still not dead. We had endured destitution, starvation, and the brutality of your soldiers. Something else was needed, the more subtle cruelty of the monk.

All in the name of the profit, your God, crucified So, you invented the Inquisition. We were heathens and impenitent. You torture us, you fling us to rot in your dungeons. You could burn us alive and all in the name of the Gospel whose only message is "Peace upon earth and good will toward men. All in the name of the profit, your God, crucified by the Inquisitors of his day.

SCENE II - TO RUSSIA WITH LOVE

ZAROAYA *(cont'd)*

The martyr—whom you have turned into a butcher. God of the Christians—they have nailed your hands and feet so you could not come to the help of the wretched—but your lips are free!

Cry out! Cry out to them these vile judges—that Hell is here. Here, where living men and women are sacrificed to your glory, here where they offer for a psalm the groans of the tormented, and for incense—the smell of burning flesh. Cry out that Hell is here! Yes—Hell with its braziers—Hell with its damned—Hell with devils. Yes, Hell—Hell is here.

(SARAH releases the character and steps forward.)

SARAH

St. Petersburg was a different story. Every night after each performance a red carpet was rolled out over the snow from the stage door to a gilded sleigh. A magnificent team of horses raced me across the snow to my hotel as adoring fans ran beside it tossing flowers. At a banquet the French Ambassador gave in my honor. I truly blushed as he raised his glass and proclaimed, "Madame, France has only one ambassador—Sarah Bernhardt!"

This was two nights after the Czar Alexander III came backstage to meet me following my performance at the Winter Palace.

THE DIVINE GOLDEN YEARS – *by Robert W. Cabell*

SARAH
I was shocked and rushed forward to make a deep curtsey when he gestured me to stop and said, "No, Madame, it is I who must bow to you." And to my amazement, he did!

(SARAH claps her hands together and flashes a triumphant smile, and then we see a sudden memory intrude and the smile slowly fades.)

SCENE III

MY GREEK TRAGEDY

SARAH
(SARAH crosses thoughtfully to her dressing table and sits, then after a moment looks up at the audience..)

The time has come to speak of my husband, Jacques Damala. I can't avoid it any longer. Sometimes there are things in our life which are hard to talk about, hard to admit, and hard to resist. Damala was all of those. My marriage was truly summed up by the title of a play by Bernard Shaw, *Don Juan in Hell,* for that is what he was, and that is where he took me.

(SARAH changes her look as she speaks. She puts her hair up in a French twis and applies blush and eyeliner and lip rouge, looking older, grander.)

At the not so tender age of thirty-eight, I fell madly in love with a twenty-six-year-old Greek diplomat and a career womanizer named Aristides Damala. The name Jacques came later, when he became my leading man. Actors; always changing names, you know. The way things look on a marquee can mean everything. But, not to avoid the subject any further, Damala was terribly handsome, a man whose reputation as a heart breaker was exceeded by reality.

I met Damala through my sister Jeanne, shortly before I departed on my European tour, and I was suspended between one breath and another when those glittering eyes undressed me with a glance that was both blasé

THE DIVINE GOLDEN YEARS – *by Robert W. Cabell*

SARAH *(cont'd)*
and blissful. He had a sensuous tremor to his upper lip that made my heart tremble in response.

Jeanne introduced him to me at my studio, and he promptly sat down and languidly removed a cigarette from a gold and jeweled case and lit it up, knowing as all Paris knew, that I never allowed anyone to smoke in front of me. But I simply looked at him and thought, 'This is the most handsome creature I have ever seen.'

His reckless romancing of the Parisian upper-class females had driven one woman to suicide and two to divorce; the French government decided it was time for Damala to fish in foreign seas, and he was sent to Russia.

(SARAH rises now with new hairstyle, jewelry and makeup and reaches for an elegant long silk evening shawl.)

Though I had so far refused any offers to perform in Russia, as soon as I heard he had been reassigned there, I changed all my plans to insert a six-month engagement in the middle of everything, just for the chance to see him again.

(Hands on hips, trailing the shawl behind her she saunters across the stage as she speaks).

To give you a measure of his charms, no sooner did he arrive in Russia than he fell into passionate liaisons with not one, but two, of Prince Rostopchin's daughters. Their royal ménage-a-trois was the scandal of Saint Petersburg!

SCENE III - MY GREEK TRAGEDY

SARAH
(She looks up and out as if she just entered.)
When I saw him after my arrival, he had a lithesome young princess decorating each arm as he crossed the royal ballroom to barely acknowledge me.
(She looks off stage right as if searching for him as she speaks.)
I was on the arm of Garnier, my current on-and-off-stage leading man. It was as if he, and in fact the world, no longer existed.
(She turns to looks at the audience.)
That is the true meaning of blind passion.
(Smiles ruefully and crosses to sit on the divan.)
My son, my friends, my critics could say anything, do anything, and I just thought—how handsome he was.
(Shrugs dejectedly.)
Damala could ignore me, debase me, slap me across the face with his infidelities, and I just thought—how handsome he was.
(She twists the ends of the shawl around each writs in frustration.)
I discarded loyal, professional actors to star opposite a rank amateur, because I thought—how handsome he was.
(She brings her hands together in her lap hold the shawl as she speaks softly.)
As many times as I had played Victor Hugo's Doña Sol opposite Sully or Angelo or Coquelin in *Hernani*, the lines of her first sweet speech had never rung so true as when I said them to Damala.

THE DIVINE GOLDEN YEARS – by Robert W. Cabell

SARAH *(as Dona Sol)*

We will leave tomorrow. Hernani, do not condemn me for my new boldness. Are you my demon or my angel? I cannot tell –

(She thrust her hands forward and pulls them apart as if they were tied or bound in love.)

but I am your slave. Wherever you go I will go. Stay or depart, - I belong to you. Why? I cannot say.

(She rises and takes an eager step towards his direction.)

I need to see you, and must have you near and have you all the time.

(She wraps the shawl around her shoulders as if she is suddenly cold and afraid.)

When the sound of your step fades, then I think that my heart has stopped its beat. You are gone, and I am gone from myself.
But no sooner does that beloved foot fall sound in my ear again, than I remember life

(She raises the silk shawl up high above her head like a fluttering banner of welcome.)

. . . and feel my soul comeback to me.

(She holds the pose for a moment and then release the character and turns sadly towards the audience.)

SARAH

Finally in 1882, *(hands on hips and glaring)* after he continued to copulate in every direction and squander my money on endless whores and mistresses, I ran away to England to marry him, because I thought—how handsome he was.

SCENE III - MY GREEK TRAGEDY

SARAH
Blind passion is living hell. But the worst thing of all—
I was blind to the obvious clues that he was a drug
addict.
(Crosses to the end of the divan and drops the shawl across the end.)
In fact, unknown to me at the time, he entered my life
as the drug supplier to my sister Jeanne who was to die
from her morphine addiction before he did. The same
addiction claimed my younger sister Regina, at the
tender age of eighteen.
(Pours herself a drink.in to a goblet)
A fact Damala never denied. Damala never denied or
made excuses for anything. As his addiction worsened,
he would simply inject himself with a syringe, right
through his clothing in mid-sentence, even while we
were entertaining!
(Begins to walk slowly back towards her dressing table, drink in hand .)
He had the disarming mixture of innocent youth and
corrupt decadence with everything he did. He had thick,
glossy waves of hair and an exquisite nose that set off
the most remarkable eyes I had ever seen.
(She stops and looks to the audience with a sigh.)
A man made for women. Made to be loved by women,
(finish crossing to her dressing table and sits.)
and as someone once said, he was Casanova and the
Marquis de Sade all rolled into one.
(Picks up a picture frame with Damala's picture in it.)
From time to time he did tell me he loved me, but in
truth, I don't think he had the capacity to love. He could
insight love, but not receive or reciprocate it.

THE DIVINE GOLDEN YEARS – by Robert W. Cabell

SARAH
(Regretfully puts the picture frame back.)
   He had a passion for me, that is true. And I had nothing but passion for him.
(Rises and crosses back to far left of divan and sits.)
   In fact, and you must not laugh at this, though throughout my life I have laughed when I should have cried and cried when I should have laughed—I was faithful to Damala.
(SARAH sets down her wine glass on the side table.)
   It's true; I had resolved to be faithful to this adulterous monster when I was unable to be faithful to any other man in my life. Blinded by love for Damala, I insisted that he play the role of Loris opposite me in Sardou's *Fedora*, which I had negotiated in my devastated garden prior to my tour and marriage.

   Sardou insisted he would not, and since a contract is a contract, I finally agreed to Sardou's terms and mounted another production in another theater for Damala to star in.

   While his production enjoyed a mild success, he was enraged by the stellar success of my *Fedora*. How he tortured and ruined me with his gambling, his mistresses, and his devastating drug infested-violence.

   After being married to Damala, I never feared dying and going to Hell, for Hell had found me first.

SCENE III - MY GREEK TRAGEDY

SARAH
>For two years I was imprisoned in Hell's darkest corner until an angel in the form Jean Richepin, furious at the abuse I had resigned myself to, literally ravished me—though in the most lovingly passionate way—back into my senses.

(Picks up another picture frame and gazes at it.)
>It was the beginning of my fight for freedom and sanity. I legally separated from Damala, although he drifted in and out of my life whenever he pleased. This of course infuriated Jean, but for the last few years Damala was so riddled and debilitated by drugs, I became not a wife but a guardian. The love of my loins became Jean Richepin, as towering a talent as he was a man.

(Puts the picture down.)
>I first met Jean in 1876, when he was very radical in his behavior. He was very ala mode, running around Paris on a new fangled mechanical contraption called a bicycle, dressed in very tight clothing that showed off his bulging muscles and made the ladies swoon wherever he went. At one time he lived with a band of gypsies in the forest of Fontainebleau. At another, he performed as a tumbler-wrestler-weight-lifter in the Neuilly Fair.

>He was loving, attentive, nurturing, and an artistic genius as a writer and poet. The reigning Prince of Bohemia, he personified the romantic vagabonds of his poems and plays. He was a vigorous breath of fresh air in my life after the drugs and madness of Damala.

THE DIVINE GOLDEN YEARS – *by Robert W. Cabell*

SARAH
So of course, I cheated on him.
(shrugs and laughs)
Constantly. *(laughs again)* I was always pleading my innocence, like Fedora pleading her love to Loris.
(Rises from the couch and moves slowly towards her dressing table.)
And Despite the tremendous box office *Fedora* was bringing in, my take was not enough to pay off the
(Sits and the table and glances in the mirror)
creditors that Damala had heaped upon me as well as the lavish life I had always maintained for my prince, Maurice.
(She gathers up several of the scattered necklaces, rings and earrings on her dressing table and places them in a small gilded box.).
I was forced to sell my precious jewels and my beautiful carriages and horses. . .
(She rises, snatches up the gilded Peacock-feather fan and saunter back to the divan..)
And take *Fedora* on tour to the European cities whose theatres had greater capacities for beaucoup box-office receipts.
(She stretches out on the divan fanning herself and gesturing with it.)
It was a whirlwind tour-de-force, on and off stage, with Jean by my side. And thank God he was, for 1883 was a very bad year. I had promised to produce and star in Richepin's play *Nana-Sahib*, an exotic mistake set in India at the time of the Sepoy Mutiny.

SCENE III - MY GREEK TRAGEDY

SARAH
Twenty actors were buried in the same plot that involved the rebel, Nana-Sahib, and his beautiful mistress, Djamma, along with a mass of courtiers, Sepoys, beggars, and British colonials.

The critics loved it, except for the fact that the actors kept getting in the way of the scenery. As if this dismal reception wasn't enough, in December that daughter of joy and sadistic ex-friend of mine, Marie Colombier?
(Tosses the fan down unceremoniously, leaps to her feet and stomps.)
She released a slanderous satire of my life, thinly veiled by the title, *The Memoirs of Sarah Barnum*. It was scabrous pornography, a depraved product of a malicious mind that excels at scatological vituperation, anti-Semitic venom, and revolting lies.
(Mimes the action.)
I stormed into Marie's apartment, brandishing a whip and a knife, with Jean at my side, ready to skin her alive. She had the foresight to flee through a door concealed behind a tapestry and save herself.

The newspapers carried the story across the Atlantic of "The Bernhardt's Attack," which had the affect of sending the sales of *Sarah Barnum* soaring. Unfortunately, it did not have the same effect on the ticket sales of *Nana-Sahib*, which we soon were forced to close. Once again, my career and finances were rescued by the creative genius of Victorien Sardou with his new play

THE DIVINE GOLDEN YEARS – by Robert W. Cabell

SARAH *(cont'd)*
Theodora, a spectacular crowd pleaser portraying the life of the Byzantine Empress, Theodora, and her intrigue and infidelities that ended in betrayal and execution. It ran for three hundred performances before it moved to London and became the smash hit of 1884.

Sadly, the joy and triumph of *Theodora* was all too quickly dispelled by the death of Victor Hugo, who was lost to us in May of 1885. On the day of his death, France, as one being with one heart, wept at the loss of our literary God. At his insistence, Hugo's body was laid to rest in a pauper's pinewood coffin. Paris mourned him as he lay in state under the Arc de Triomphe before he was taken in an unadorned hearse to his final resting place.

As I walked behind his coffin I remembered my early career. I debuted in 1863, at eighteen, in the world's most prestigious theater, the Comédie-Française. Unfortunately, I did not last the year, after hitting one of their Grand-dames, Madame Nathalie. The cow shoved my little sister, Regina, into a pillar for stepping on her dress train, and bloodied Regina's nose—so I slapped her soundly and was expelled.

I then joined the Gymnase Theater, where at a command performance - I proceeded to insult the Emperor. I ignorantly reciting two Victor Hugo poems—who was then living in exile for his literary attacks against the Emperor—. *(Shrugs)*

SCENE III - MY GREEK TRAGEDY

SARAH

I managed to arrive at my twentieth birthday, at the end of 1864, an unwed mother of the illegitimate son of a Belgian prince—and out of work! Things could have been better. But in 1866, I was blessed with an offer to join the Odeon Theater, and my career took a positive turn—until what you now known as the Franco-Prussian War. In 1870, I played the real life role of a war nurse at a makeshift hospital we set up in the Odeon Theater.

No death scene or dramatic play could ever equal the Dantesque reality of the living hell of war. I will never shake the horror of gleaning the battlefield at night for sparks of life in a few wounded soldiers to carry them back to the hospital, or simply hold their hands until they died. Years later, when I played Napoleon's nineteen year old son in *L'Aiglon* by Edmond Rostand, I would call upon those memories again and again.

(Everywhere there are whispers of men who are dying as Sarah draws a sword and holds it aloft.)

SARAH *(as the Duke)*

Ah, now I understand, his dying cry came to this plain that knows such cries by heart. Like the first line of an old song and when the man's voice stops the plain goes on! I understand! Death-rattle, groan and cry are Wagram's memories, murmured aloud!

THE DIVINE GOLDEN YEARS – by Robert W. Cabell

SARAH *(as the Duke cont'd)*

He does not move—oh, let me get away! He really seems to have fallen in the battle! It must be like that—that coat—that blood—another! And another, there! And there! Everywhere stretched the same blue shapes. They are dying, they are dying so for leagues!

(Whispers of death and dying.)

We think the ground will keep our secrets, but the plain can tell its memories and tonight the very earth cries out!

All the plain is waving with a forest of arms and I am treading on a field of uniforms. I've slipped upon a sword belt. Where shall I turn, oh horrible crippled, dying ghosts, your feverish eyes terrifying me. But you are glorious, your France is proud of your heroic names. Poor unknown names! Inglorious names of men who forge a nation's glory!

(She lowers the sword slowly to release the moment.)

SARAH

When the war ended, we lost face, two million francs, and our Emperor to Germany. And my life began anew, a new life with Victor Hugo. I played the Little Queen in *Ruy Blas* under his direction, and my life and my career were elevated to the heavens.

(She replaces the sword in the brass umbrella stand.)

SCENE III - MY GREEK TRAGEDY

SARAH

Hugo was in the front row on the night I first performed Doña Sol in *Hernani* opposite Mount Sully. I realized the success of that the following morning,
(She steps to her dressing table and picks up a letter.)
when I received a small box with the accompanying note:
(She reads the letter as we hear the voice of Hugo.)

HUGO *(Voice from off stage)*

Madame, you were great and charming; you moved me, me the old warrior, and, at a certain moment when the public, touched and enchanted by you, applauded, I wept. This tear which you caused me to shed is yours. I place it at your feet, . . . Victor Hugo.

SARAH

Hugo's "tear" was a perfect tear-shaped diamond drop delicately suspended on a gold chain bracelet. To say I treasured it would be a slight to the immensity of that emotion. I was inconsolable years later when I lost it at the country estate of the Sassoon's in England. M. Sassoon was so moved by my distress, he sent me a magnificent jewel to replace it, but sadly I returned it to him explaining that no jewel, no matter how magnificent, could ever take the place of Victor Hugo's tear.

(She lovingly slips the letter back into the envelope and kisses it.)

THE DIVINE GOLDEN YEARS – *by Robert W. Cabell*

SARAH
At his graveside, with a veil to hide my tears, I said my final goodbye.
(She silently puts the letter away, and then silently walks back to the end of the couch and sits. She picks up a picture frame again and looks at it sadly for a moment.)
Three years later I would also bury Damala, whom I had gone to great lengths to save. When news reached me that Damala was not only penniless, but a complete physical wreck, I went to him at once. It was the last straw for Richepin. Jean broke off our affair for the last time, but remained forever my faithful and loving friend. There was nothing else I could do.

Both of my sisters were morphine maniacs and died the same way that Damala was soon to die. I could not let him suffer through that in some dank abandoned room or in some twisted garbage strewn alley. I placed him in a fine sanatorium and visited him daily. He died from drugs at the age of thirty-four, and quand méme, in spite of everything, I loved him.

Throughout my marriage, throughout the rest of my life, my career kept going. Nothing stopped or interfered with that, for I was nothing if I was not an actress. Before food or water, before air itself, I needed to act.

SCENE IV

EVER ONWARD

SARAH

> I needed to get away. I needed to make vast amounts of money to cover my uncontrollable spending, which was the morphine of my life. Women everywhere understand that when things get tough, the tough go shopping.
>
> My American impresario, Edward Jarrett, was always ready with a grand tour and pots of gold whenever I needed one, and this time it took me to South America.
>
> In Brazil, *Theodora* was so spellbinding; the church actually accused me of witchcraft, which worked like magic on the box office.
>
> The night of *Theodora's* first performance in Rio, the *(She raises her arms up and out as if receiving the accolades of a crowd.)*
>> house erupted into an uncontrollable hysteria of flowers, gloves, fans, and hats raining down upon us as they demanded one hundred curtain calls. I was summoned to the imperial box where dear Dom Pedro, the Emperor of Brazil, presented me with a gold bracelet that literally took my breath away—and I fainted on the spot!

THE DIVINE GOLDEN YEARS – *by Robert W. Cabell*

SARAH

On a later South American tour, I brought *La Tosca*, Sardou's greatest creation for me, to the same theater. When Tosca agrees to give herself to Count Scarpia in return for the life and freedom of her love, Mario, you can sense the deadly intent that lies latent in the scene. She demands he give the orders to save him in front of her, and before she surrenders, insists he write the letter of safe passage.

As he signs the note with his last stroke, she plunges a dagger, to the hilt, into his back. He staggers, clutching at her in deathly rage, until he finally dies, and she rushes off to save her lover. By this time, she is getting a bit hysterical.

SARAH *(as Tosca)*

Mario, my love, very soon we shall be far from this horrible place. Capitan Spoletta has orders to lead you out as if to execution, but the guns will be charged with powder only. You must fall as if shot, the soldiers will be sent away, and the gates will be open to us. Soon shall we be far from the power of these wretches. On the high seas they cannot harm us. The whole thing will take but five minutes, my love. Act your part well. At the first shot, fall down. Spoletta leads my beloved Mario away as I wait outside the wall of the terrace. Surely with the post-horses we will find along the route we can be at

SCENE IV - EVER ONWARD

SARAH *(as Tosca cont'd)*

Civitavecchia in four hours. Oh God, when I see the coastline of Italy fading in the distance—what a relief.

(Listens for a moment.)

Ah, I hear them walking up there on the terrace... They have stopped. This is the moment. What are they waiting for? A delay might be fatal. It is awful—this waiting. It frays your nerves. Even though it is only a game the thought that they are shooting at him—ah, my god get on with it. Get on with it. Let it be over.

(She hears a gunshot and screams.)

Ahh—! It is over. Let us go now. Ah, I almost forgot his cloak.

(She takes Marios' cloak and rushes into the courtyard to his side as he lays face down, hands sprawling to his side.)

It is me. Do not move. There is a soldier passing. Wait! Good—he has gone. Here is your cloak now! Quick! To your feet.

(She rushes to the side and peers off to see if it is clear.)

Quickly now! Come on get up! Do you not hear me Mario?

(She kneels.)

Blood?!! He is dead. My Marios is dead! Assassin! Assassins, you were supposed to have save him.

(She breaks the moment and turns to the audience.)

THE DIVINE GOLDEN YEARS – *by Robert W. Cabell*

SARAH
    Etc. etc. etc. Then, she hurls herself out of the tower to a certain death below.
(She rises and brushes off her dress and speaks matter-of-factly.)
    On that particular night in Rio, the mattress that always broke my fall was not placed in position, and I came crashing down onto a bare wooden stage floor, smashing my knee. I was in hideous pain and hobbled through the next few performances.
(She rises and brushes off her dress.)
    But, everyone was so kind to me in South America. The Argentinean government granted me 13,000 acres of land—exactly where that abundance of acreage was I never quite found out. When news reached Peru, I arrived there to find a carload of guano dung for fertilizing it awaiting me as a gift. How thoughtful. It is nice to know what people really think of you.

The Peruvian Indian priests also honored me with a macabre treasure, an ancient necklace created by a secret process that looked like a string of pearls. It turned out to be a rope of petrified human eyes. I was delighted.

Uruguay was not as accommodating. I asked if they couldn't put on a little revolution for my entertainment, but the government failed to comply.

SCENE IV - EVER ONWARD

SARAH
This was about the time Jarrett decided to drop dead of a heart attack in Montevideo.

My trust and admiration of Edward Jarrett was inestimable. He had been to me in business what my little lady was to me in my life, my rock and foundation.

I'm sure I seemed cold and aloof to my company as I dissolved inside, standing by his grave. The diatribe of tears that came so convincingly to me on stage was never available to me in life. Reality was always too deep and bleak for tears.

SCENE V

A THEATER OF MY OWN

SARAH

I was done with South America. I wanted my son, my home, and my close circle of friends and artistic associates, my little court as I called it. It included such dignitaries and visionaries as the Prince of Wales and the lovely Princess Alexandria, Victor Hugo, Louis Pasteur, Oscar Wilde, Theodore Roosevelt, my ever-present Jojotte, George Clarin, Gustave Flaubert, and the phenomenal composer, Rossini. Most of my pets I kept at my fortress home of Belle Ilse, but my little favorites stayed in Paris.

I was, always had been, and always would be an original personality and talent. I had to do things both on and off stage my own way. So in 1893, fed up with the management of others, I dissolved all my partnerships and agreements and leased the Theater de la Renaissance as its sole producer and director.

I ran my company with a field marshal's efficiency and created my productions with the splendor of an Empress. And I was blessed with drawing some of the greatest new talent of that era into the fold of my company during the five years I occupied the Renaissance Theater.

One of my great leading men was Édouard de Max. He appeared heroically virile as Mark Antony onstage, but was a slinky little Cleopatra off.

SCENE V

A THEATER OF MY OWN

SARAH

De Max was an assemblage of the exotic and the extraordinary, both physically and sexually. A notorious homosexual, he would entertain a bevy of naked apostles in his own private Roman bath, allowing them the privilege of viewing him naked in a Nero-sized marble bath of rose water. He would then hurl gold coins at his nude admirers from a Byzantine bronze bowl he kept by his side to signal the commencement of the more debauched moments of his personal Bacchanalian festivities.

He was a total scamp and made me laugh constantly. He pulled stunts like turning his back to the audience at the final moment of one of my legendary death scenes and flashing me a smile of blackened teeth that would send me into gales of laughter as the curtain descended.

I have noticed that homosexuals tend to run in packs, and they tend to run around me. De Max and his little "Maxies" were better feminine companions than most actresses.

And it is not true that I was petty and jealous of younger female talent. I tried to be a friend and mentor to Eleonora Duse. However, Eleonora and her manager seemed to find it necessary to try to topple and replace me. I extended an invitation for her to perform in Paris, and to my surprise she chose three of my standard repertoire.

THE DIVINE GOLDEN YEARS – *by Robert W. Cabell*

SARAH

This gorgeous creature, who was making a sensation in the theatrical world for her poetic simplicity and naturalism, decided to perform the role of Marguerite in *La Dame aux Camélias* at the same time I was. It was an obvious attempt—as she was fifteen years younger than I and much more lovely—to outshine me. Fortuitously, the critics found her a pale comparison, as she lacked, and let me quote, the "brilliant showmanship," of my interpretation; and she received no acclaim. The poor child went into one of her epic states of despair. She was much more of a drama queen off stage than she was on, and she went sulking back to Italy.

Meanwhile, I moved into the "Sarah Bernhardt Theater," which was one of the most opulent theatrical houses in history, with yellow velvet and brocades and ivory or white woodwork augmented by Lalique. Très formidable. I was fifty-five, looked thirty-five, and signed a twenty-five year lease.

SCENE VI

LAST LOVER

SARAH

To count a woman's age or the number of her lovers is the height of vulgarity. I have had only a few great loves in my life. Kiertary was my first great love. He was a gallant army officer in whose bed I lost my virginity, and who proved tremendously helpful in 1870 when I opened my hospital at the Odeon.

And George Hass, now *there* was a mover and a shaker, and he moved and shook me more than once. We had the same colored hair, the same color eyes, and the same taste in makeup—although his was a little more excessive than mine. But don't let the mascara fool you; what a man! He was perhaps the first man I fell in love with. He was extremely sophisticated, the best dressed man in Paris, and sadly a man of many mistresses who grew tired of my little jealous games.

And Mount-Sully, the Adonis of Paris theater, and my leading man on and off stage at the Comédie-Française, had the body of a god and the intellect of an ant.

I made love to all my leading men, even Lou Tellegen, the last amour to occupy my heart and bed. He played Essex to my Elizabeth in a film I made in 1912. Lou was tall, with gloriously chiseled features, muscular, and eager to please me in any way I wanted. And let me tell you, I wanted—even though I was sixty-something—I still wanted. The minute my eyes landed on his—I wanted.

THE DIVINE GOLDEN YEARS – *by Robert W. Cabell*

SARAH
But my most notable relationship, next to my husband Damala, was Prince Henri Antoine de Ligne, who was the father of my son. I fascinated and delighted him until I announced my pregnancy. After that, I didn't see him for many years… nor did my son.

One of my favorite roles was Adrienne in Augustin Eugene Scribe and Ernest Wilfried Legouvé's, *Adrienne Lecouvreur*, who was a famous actress before my time. Her lover was Maurice, a nobleman above her station in life, and she was poisoned by an adulterous princess and rival for his affections. Every time I did that role, I thought of Henri when I started the scene where the poison makes her hallucinate.

SARAH *(as Adrienne)*

No! No! Not now, I am well here.
(Touches her heart.)
But there is a strange sensation here.
(Touches her head.)
Very strange; a thousand fantastic objects seem to pass before me, without any order or connection. Where are we? My imagination seems to be wandering. I lose all power of controlling it. Ah! I know where I am. I am in the theater! Maurice will be there—the house will be full, very full, but for me there will be only one object—Maurice! Still—still applause is pleasant.

SCENE VI - LAST LOVER

SARAH *(as Adrienne cont'd)*

The play will soon begin, and they are anxious. No doubt—for they have been promised for so long a time, the psyche of "Corneille" —for a very long time—from the days when I first saw Maurice. Maurice has never said to me "I love you" and I have never said so much to him. The words spring from my heart to my lips, but I dare not utter them.

Now in this piece—in this psyche—there are certain lines that I can address to him before everybody and nobody will find me out. It is a good thought—is it not? What was that voice? Hush! Hush! I must appear on stage. What a splendid audience!—How numerous—how brilliant, how my movements are followed by every glance. They are kind, very kind. Very kind to love me in this way. But where is he?

Oh—yonder in his box. Yes, yes! There is Maurice—he smiles at me. Don't turn from me those eyes that wound me.

Those kind, yet piercing, loving eyes which seem to share in the emotion they raise in me. Alas! The more dangerous they look the more fondly do I gaze at them. What heavenly power, which I can't understand, urges me to say more than I ought to say.

THE DIVINE GOLDEN YEARS – *by Robert W. Cabell*

SARAH *(as Adrienne cont'd)*

I whom shame should at least compel to wait, till you love, had explained your emotions. You sigh, my lord, and I too, do sigh. Like myself, you seem amazed. Tis my duty to keep silent, tis yours to find words. And yet, it is I who speaks first.

(She just sits silent for a moment lost in thought and then looks up at the audience and shrugs.)

SARAH

One evening when I returned to my dressing room after a performance of Adrienne, I thought I was hallucinating when a fifty-year-old, but ever elegant, Prince Henri Antoine de Ligne, entered my dressing room. I had not seen the father of my son for two decades.

'You look well Henri, but after all these years, what has moved you to pay me a visit?'

"Why should I be the only one not to come and applaud the great Sarah Bernhardt? I read about you all the time. You and... I read about you and... our son."

'Ah...' I said. 'So, it is time that you finally meet, no? I am glad for both of you. Come to lunch with us tomorrow, Henri, he is so much like you. Twenty-one, and he has all of your magnificent charm.'

SCENE VI - LAST LOVER

SARAH

He smiled at my complement and thanked me humbly—something else I had never seen—then he left. The next day, you could sense Henri's instant admiration for his son with his elegance and manners, witty repartee, and graceful ease in what must have been a tense and awkward situation. Henri grew silent and studied Maurice for a moment before he said, "Do you know who I am to you?"

With his usual grace and dignity my little prince replied, "Mother spoke your name when she introduced you, and the rest sir, is no great secret."

Henri smiled sadly, and then continued, "I did not expect to find you as you are, so charming and understanding. I am a widower and am therefore free… now that I have seen you, I wish…to recognize you and to offer you my name, my title, and in later years, my wealth, which would legally be yours."

Maurice thought, but only for a moment. Then he shook his head, and over a cup of tea, told his father he could not accept.

So Henri naturally asked, "Why not?"

Maurice replied, "Sir, it is very kind of you to offer me such an honor. There are only a few princes of Europe, but there is only one Sarah Bernhardt, and she has only one son, and I consider *that* the greater honor."

THE DIVINE GOLDEN YEARS – *by Robert W. Cabell*

SARAH
 Henri bowed to his son. "I understand your feelings. They do you honor."

(Sarah smiles to herself then looks back to the audience.)

 The only constant love throughout my life, was my son Maurice.

 Did I tell you my little prince married a real princess? Princess Terka of Poland. My son, who had been denied by his father and sadly ignored, no, played second fiddle to my career, had grown up handsome and fiercely devoted to me in spite of everything.

 We spoiled each other with love and drained each other of money. But I could never imagine my life without him. Acting was my life, but it was Maurice who gave me a soul.

(Sits down upon the trunk.)

 But I have yet to mention my greatest love aside from my son—in fact, my shadow. I don't mean this in a narcissistic way, I mean this love was an everyday part of my life for forty years, a mere extension of myself, always there, always treasured—my "little lady." Only death separated us, and there has never been a day since in my life where I have not needed and ached for her.

SCENE VI - LAST LOVER

SARAH

Her name was Madame Guérard, and she gave me unconditional love from the day I first met her when I arrived, an awkward and bony girl, at the apartments of my gloriously beautiful mother. She was a great courtesan of Paris, who lived along with my two gorgeous, younger half-sisters that had never left her side.

Both possessed a beauty I could never equal in a world where beauty was all. Until the age of fifteen, I had spent my life in boarding schools and convents paid for by my Catholic father and was ignorant of all the realities of Mother's life.

My little lady lived above us and served as a nurse for our household. She knew how I ached for maternal love and attention.

This was never to be available to me from my own mother, but thank God for the haven she provided me upstairs in her home. It was there I confessed my deepest longings and darkest secrets, vented my frustrations, and cried away my anger and sorrow.

She took me under her wing and kept me there for the rest of her life.

(Sighs and crosses herself.)

THE DIVINE GOLDEN YEARS – *by Robert W. Cabell*

SARAH

My little lady… what a vestige of goodness and beauty! (*Sarah crosses herself and touches her locket.*)

She had an endless, inexhaustible supply of it, until the day she died, a day unequaled in all the sorrows my life has ever known. She had always been my emotional haven, like Belle Isle was my physical haven.

SCENE VII

MY ISLAND PARADISE

SARAH

Belle Isle was my own personal island paradise, and one I shared with my family and dearest friends every summer for the last thirty years of my life.

Belle Isle had two conflicting faces, like far too many people I know. On the Atlantic side there were jagged cliffs, cleft by the hammer of God. They sheered straight down to the ocean below, with endless raging waves battering the rocks that skirted them.

Once you passed through the inner reefs to the interior of the island, you were greeted by the most picturesque pastoral utopia of gentle valleys and rolling hills, dotted with doll-like cottages.

Tucked away on the promontory of my island Shangri-La, right where the winds converged to blow their mightiest blows, stood an old, fierce, and medieval fortress. It was uninhabitable, inhospitable, and inaccessible. I simply had to have it. It was my castle, and I was the queen of the 16th-century fortress whose main entrance was approached by a small drawbridge. Quell ambience!

It had the most massive fireplace you have ever seen. I populated the hall with over-stuffed couches and chairs, then scattered the floors with rugs of fur and Persian decent, and covered the walls with a cornucopia of masks, primitive art, and garish, but glorious, paintings.

THE DIVINE GOLDEN YEARS – *by Robert W. Cabell*

SARAH
> The coup d'état was to herbalize it with pots, vats, and vases of plants and flowers everywhere you looked. With all that restoration and decorating, I was bitten by the artistic bug and took up the hammer and attacked the stone to release a piece of art I could see imprisoned inside. I reveled in the dust, sweat, and dirt of physical exertion to leave a tactile, tangible, sculpted piece of art that would endure beyond my life—the constant dream of all actors. The play I so often performed based on the famous actress, Adrienne Lecouvreur, expressed the frustration of all actors; that there is nothing left of our work or artistry after the curtain comes down.

SARAH *(as Adrienne Lecouvreur)*

> Oh! Theatrical triumph! My heart beats no more with those ardent emotions! And you, long studies of an art that I loved so much—nothing will remain of you after I am gone. Nothing lives of us after our death, nothing but recollection.

SARAH
> My most indelible memory of Belle Isle was right after the sun had set and the sea went glassy calm. As the sun retreated, the water turned from aqua to azure blue, and the smells from dinner came wafting out from underneath the covered dishes as the table was being set. The men gathered, decked out in white twill slacks

SCENE VII - MY ISLAND PARADISE

SARAH
and jackets, and the women seemed to float in tea dresses, all in shades of pale pastels, and wide-brimmed straw hats. Gales of childish giggles and laughter serenaded me. Maurice and my grandchildren, with their playmates, fed carrots and lump sugar to my two horses, Cassis and Vermouth. Or they chased the dogs about the yard and rode in our little donkey cart until they were begrudgingly captured and dragged to the table for grace and the evening meal. A blissful, serene assemblage of loved ones all lulled into peaceful, satiated happiness.

SCENE VIII

THE LAST LEG

SARAH

Achilles had his heel, and I had my knee. After *Tosca* in 1905, my knee grew worse and worse with every passing year. By 1915, I could suffer no more—no, I could live no more—with such agony. I needed to be divorced from my knee, but no one would operate on me, They were afraid to be called "The Butcher of Bernhardt," or worse yet, that I would not survive. They did not care how I was suffering!

Finally, a plucky little doctor from Bordeaux, out of either great kindness or temporary insanity, agreed to "do the dirty deed." I was so relieved, I was the one cheering my family up as they gathered around me, sobbing before the operation.

(Laughs.)

I sang *"La Marseillaise"* as they wheeled me into the operating room, because I was soon to be free of pain!

Like a woman who loses 185 pounds of fat when she divorces her husband, I lost twenty-five pounds at least when I divorced my leg—and almost as much aggravation. I was seventy-one years old; I was not going to run a race or take another lover. I loved to sit by the sea or in my garden with my grandchild, Lysiane, by my side. Of course, after three months of that sort of nonsense, I was back performing!

SCENE VIII - THE LAST LEG

SARAH

Artificial legs, no matter how many I tried, were too awkward and uncomfortable. I hadn't cut off the real thing to be tortured and annoyed by a cheap imitation! I was either carried around in a petite chair with poles, like Cleopatra on a budget, or carried in the arms of a man—something I had still not lost my taste for.

With the first news of World War I, I arranged to be carried down to the front to perform for the troops. My leg was gone, but not my voice; it was still strong, golden, young, and beautiful—even if I was not. And I could drown out the blare of cannons and gunfire with the thunder of my voice.

I returned to my apartment in Paris on the Boulevard Pereire after the war, and found my home in shambles and Maurice deeper in debt. I had to use everything I left to pay it all off. Once again, I needed to make more money. I performed in plays, made six more films, and made another lucky tour to my beloved London.

In the autumn of 1922, little Sacha Guitry, all grown up, had written a play for me that I loved, but I began suffering from fainting spells during rehearsals and had to withdraw from the production.

I thought I was feeling better when he offered me a part in a picture he'd written that we decided to film right here in my apartment. But today, as we started with me seated, in my makeup, doing a scene where I play cards, I saw the cards blur and everything went black. I awoke

THE DIVINE GOLDEN YEARS – by Robert W. Cabell

SARAH
> to a priest and all my beloved ones gathered around me, with the scent of wildflowers like a mist surrounding me. They wept and cried, and I told them how much I loved them. Of all the roles over the years, it was Gilbert from Henri Meilhac's *Frou-frou*, which was Gilbert's nickname to those who loved her, that seemed to reflect my death the closest of all the many, many death scenes I had ever played.
>
> But this time it was truly I, who lay dying.

SARAH *(as Gilbert)*

> I pass away amid my loved ones, tranquil, happy. Sartoris, there is no need for forgiveness. Forgiveness for what? Loving me too much? This was my misfortune. Everyone loved me too much and because of this I die—and because of this I die so gently.
>
> Ah—Is this death? Kind heaven? How little it seems to me! Louise – where are you, Louise? Come close, that I may whisper to you. When I am dead, you must make me beautiful as I was. Not this black dress—no! You must take from among my ball dresses, a white one—the skirt is all covered with little roses. That is the one I want, and you shall see how pretty I shall look, and how once again you will find Frou-frou.

SCENE VIII - THE LAST LEG

(She turns, very tired, very sadly, to audience.)

SARAH
It is time to take my last exit.
(Laughs gently.)
It is time to bid you all...
(She blows a kiss.)
...adieu.

(Fade to black.)

END OF SHOW

SARAH IN HER DIVINE GOLDEN ROLES

SARAH *(as Fedora)*

SARAH IN HER DIVINE GOLDEN ROLES

SARAH *(as Marguerite)*

SARAH IN HER DIVINE GOLDEN ROLES

SARAH *(as Zoraya)*

SARAH IN HER DIVINE GOLDEN ROLES

SARAH *(as The Little Queen)*

SARAH IN HER DIVINE GOLDEN ROLES

SARAH *(as Dona Sol)*

SARAH IN HER DIVINE GOLDEN ROLES

SARAH *(as Theodora)*

SARAH IN HER DIVINE GOLDEN ROLES

SARAH *(as the Duke)*

SARAH IN HER DIVINE GOLDEN ROLES

SARAH *(as Tosca)*

SARAH IN HER DIVINE GOLDEN ROLES

SARAH *(as Adrienne Lecouvreur)*

SARAH IN HER DIVINE GOLDEN ROLES

SARAH *(as Frou Frou)*

www.ingramcontent.com/pod-product-compliance
Lightning Source LLC
Chambersburg PA
CBHW060149050426
42446CB00013B/2743